Big Black Creek

Vol. III

Early History of Denmark Community

Stories of Early Families

Churches of Denmark

Big Black Creek Vol. 3
Written by Billy King

Copyright © 2015
First Edition – First Printing March 2015
Library of Congress Number pending
ISBN # 978-1-939999-24-5

Published by Main Street Publishing, Inc., Jackson, TN.
Copy Editing by Shari B Yetto
Cover Design by Shari B Yetto
Edited by Billy King
Printed and bound by NetPub, Poughkeepsie, NY.

For more information write Main Street Publishing, Inc.,
206 East Main St., Suite 207, P.O. Box 696, Jackson, TN 38302
Phone 1-731-427-7379 or toll free 1-866-457-7379.
E-mail: editor@mainstreetpublishing.com for managing editor and
        lanewble@mainstreetpublishing.com for customer service.
Visit us at www.mainstreetpublishing.com and www.mspbooks.com.

Big Black Creek
Vol. III

Early History of Denmark
Community Stories of Early
Families Churches of Denmark

By Billy King

This Book is dedicated to

Mrs. Louise Stevens

Billy King

Mrs. Louise Stevens

This book is dedicated to Mrs. Louise Stevens, it would not have been possible with out her research and filing all the great history of Denmark, Tennessee

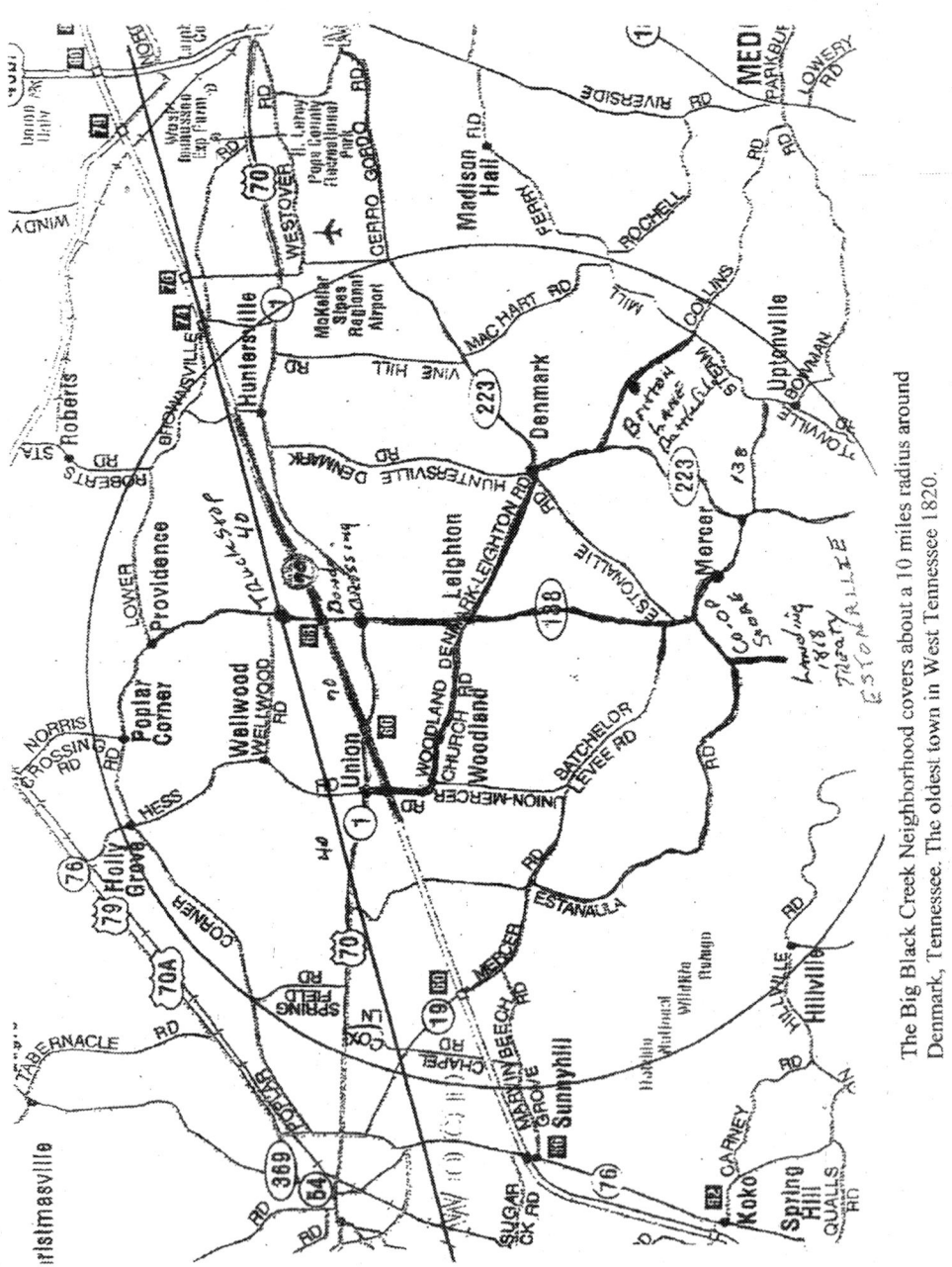

The Big Black Creek Neighborhood covers about a 10 miles radius around Denmark, Tennessee. The oldest town in West Tennessee 1820.

Early History and Stories of The Big Black Creek Community

By Mr. Fonville Neville and Billy King

Local Historian Fonville NeVille

"Mr. Fonville," as he was so fondly called by friends and neighbors, was born Howard Fonville NeVille on December 23, 1887. He was born in Nashville, Tennessee, where his father Professor Howard Casement NeVille, was a professor and treasurer at Roger Williams University. This Baptist university was founded to educate freedmen and was located at the present site of George Peabody College at Vanderbilt University. As a baby, Fonville and his mother, Mary Lydie Fonville, returned to live in Denmark with her relatives while his father taught school in Arkansas and Mississippi. Fonville had a younger sister, Dorothy Neville Keelen. As a young man, Fonville became a traveling telegraph operator for the NC & St. L Railroad. His letters home depict a young man homesick for his family and community Returning home, Fonville became a rural mail carrier for Denmark Route 2 and he continued to serve the community in this role for many years. He married Annie Laurie Duncan, who later was the first female postmaster at the Denmark Post Office. They had two daughters, Mary Jane and Julia Catherine NeVille. Fonville was a longtime member of the Denmark Presbyterian Church and, along with several generations of his family are buried in the Denmark Presbyterian Cemetery.

Local history was his passion. The Civil War had brought tragedy to the community. The Battle of Britton's Lane was a frequent topic of his ancestors and community members. He wanted to preserve these stories. Later came World War II and he carried the letters of servicemen to homes where it was necessary for him to read some of the letters to the families. Continuing to write through about rural life the years some of his writings were published under Paul Flower's column Green House in the *Memphis Commercial Appeal.* Flowers published Fonville's stories under the pen name "Ole Timer." The two men became and remained close friends.

Fonville Neville was five years old when this family portrait was taken. His father, H. C. Neville was affectionately called "Papa Bill" by his family and close friends. Eliza was paralyzed on the left side when Fonville was four but continued to keep house for the family.

Courtesy Jane Neville Hardee, Jackson, Tennessee

Four Generations

**Maggie Glass Dickinson, Rosa Dickinson King,
John Spencer (Jack) King
Billy Joe King**

Billy J. King

"Mr. Billy," was born in Bemis, Tennessee, October 29, 1937. He went to school in Bemis and, after serving in the army in Korea , he came home and went to Bethel University. He married Judy Ann Forrest of Mercer, Tennessee. After school he went into the insurance business, first in Jackson, then Memphis and spent 22 years in Louisiana, where he owned The Louisiana Agencies. After Judy's death in 1997, he sold his insurance business and went to work for the State of Louisiana at a historic site, Kent House, the oldest standing house in Alexandria, Louisiana. This sparked his interest in history. He had helped organize "Save The School," in LeCompte , Louisiana. This project was to save a school built in 1924, the project has been very successful and the school was saved and is now a community center and library for the Town of Lecompte, Louisiana, it is on the National Register of History Places.. After Judy's death, who was Professor of Nursing at Louisiana College, he moved to Alexandria, Louisiana and became the President of the Garden District Neighbor Hood Association serving until he moved back to Tennessee in 2004 to a old family farm in Denmark,

Tennessee. While Mr. King was president the entire Garden District of Alexandria was placed on the National Register of Historic Places. Mr. King s family first helped settle Denmark/Woodland in 1826. Mr. Bill has been a church organist since he was 14. He serves on several boards, The Tennessee Preservation Trust, The Carnegie for History and Arts and serves as advisor for several projects, West Bemis Elementary, Bemis Museum, and Heritage Center in Haywood County. He helped organize The Big Black Creek Historical Association to preserve the history of the Denmark, Mercer, Leighton and Woodland Communities. He has published two books, Big Black Creek, Vol. I and Big Black Creek, Vol. II "Community at War." www.bigblackcreekhistorical.com

* * *

The following stories depict the history and events of a once prosperous but fading Southern village in the rural south that is no more.

The Big Black Creek head waters start from natural springs about 5 miles north of Denmark and form a running creek at Denmark Bottoms. These ancient bubbling springs date back more than 2,000 years. The Chickasaw Indians first discovered these springs. They referred to West Tennessee, "as the land that weeps too much." The early settlers also used the springs for fresh water, stopping as they followed the Estonallie Indian Trail. The Big Black Creek flows in the Hatchie River at the Estonallie Landing.

After the signing of the Treaty in 1818 between Andrew Jackson and the Chickasaw Indians a surveyor found John Rose living near the springs. He told the surveyors that the Chickasaw called this spot Den Mark because there were animal dens in the area and they used it as a hunting ground. We now know that they had a village in the area as early as 1,000 AD. It is a dig site now of Memphis State University and they are carbon dating the finds.

Three Meriwether brothers came in about 1820. Two Reid brothers built a water mill on the banks of Big Black and Bill and John Harbert erected a trading post on it banks, they later moved the post to Denmark when it began to grow. When the early settlers started gathering for worship, this was one of the favorite spots, since there was fresh cool spring water. They would built a brush arbor and hold worship on its banks. Two of the first churches were Denmark Presbyterian and the Big Black Creek Baptist, both around 1820.

After the Harbert Brothers moved their trading post

to Denmark, it was decided to send Bill to St. Louis to buy goods for the post. Bill was single young man. He went down to Estonallie and boarded a steamboat, and it was a gambling boat. Bill soon got into a game and lost all the stores money. He persuaded the steam boat captain to write his brother telling him he had fallen overboard and drowned. Upon hearing of his brother's death, John decided to have a mock funeral. He had a coffin made and one night rang the Denmark church bell. He had six slaves carry the coffin in one door of the church and out the other. Then over to the Big Black Creek Cemetery to bury the empty coffin, but just as they got ready to bury the coffin, Bill appeared. It is suspected that all along Dan knew Bill was not dead. Bill married Mary Waddell and built a new home in Denmark. That house is still standing next to the Denmark Post Office. This is one of Denmark's most interesting stories; Dr. James Harbert Wooten, Jr. presented this information before the Colorado Co., TX. Historical Commission, Eagle Lake, Texas, March 27, 1980. Some of this history we had already discovered.

Mr. Fonville first told this story and it was just passed down, but now we know it was true from the story you are about to read.

PART OF COMMEMORATION — The home of Fonville Neville in Denmark, built in 1851, is one of the homes which will be open to the public Sunday during the Commemoration services of the Civil War Battle of Britton Lane, Madison County's largest engagement during that war. The house, built before the Civil War, is one of the oldest houses still standing in Madison County.

" ......John Harbert, b. 1797, had married Narcissa Cherry rather early after the move to Denmark, Tn. (from Sparta, White Co. TN.) but William, John's brother who was born Dec. 22, 1794, did not marry until Dec. 31, 1829, when he was 35 years old. His bride was 19 year old Mary Waddell of N. C. The rest of the 12 children of Thomas and Sarah Crockett Harbert had also moved to the Madison Co., area of TN. except for Crockett who moved just across the state line to Marshall. Co. Mississippi. Note, David Crocket was their cousin.

John and William continued to increase their land holdings, which included some acreage in Tunica Co, MS (south of Memphis, TN). Family legend tells of Stephen Harbert, who worked for his two, John and William, brothers, joining his cousin Davy Crockett, on his trip to Texas in 1835 on his way to the Alamo, down the Mississippi River as far as Tunica County, where he (Stephen) left him (Davy) to manage his brother's property in the Mississippi Valley. Stephen became famous as the champion rail splitter of the Mississippi Valley. When Stephen was 33 and was still living in Denmark, TN. he married 20 year old Nancy Vincent of North Carolina.

John and William's partnership continued to

prosper, and according to the autobiography of James A Harbert, William's fifth child, they eventually became millionaires with the store in Denmark, land in Tennessee and Mississippi, and a large number of slaves.

However, the trouble with the northern states over protective tariffs for manufactured goods, of which the South produced very little, and the question of free and slave states, made the future of the Herbart's enterprises uncertain in a border state. William decided to sell out and move to Texas, where he knew he would be far removed from possible trouble

After the death of his mother, Sallie Crockett Harbert, on 15 Sep. 1854, William, his family and 130 slaves, his brothers Stephen & Crockett and his sisters, Nancy, Sallie and their families started out on the long and difficult trip to Texas in a mule-drawn wagon train Sallie and Elizabeth were widows. It is estimated that approximately 200 people were in this group. William had offered each slave his freedom before he began the journey, since no one would have wanted a malcontent on such a trip, but they all decided to go with him.

The wagon train crossed the Mississippi River at Memphis on a ferry, then angled southwest to Little Rock, on down through Washington. Arkansas.

As soon as William arrived, he set to work purchasing 773 acres of land at a cost of $15,460. This was 1855. He eventually ended up owning 3,000 acres in the John Hadden League. William and Mary Waddell Harbert made their first land purchase in 1855, he built a house for his family and built twenty cabins for the slaves, each cabin having a brick chimney made from bricks fired in a brickyard on the place. He built a cotton gin, a two story brick smokehouse still standing today, a tanyard, and in 1857 a brick store in Columbus, Texas. Brother Stephen was in charge of all the building and he built a Baptist Church which was also used as a school house.

The agricultural census of 1860 showed that William cultivated 850 acres and had an additional 1850 in pasture. When Texas seceded from the Union on March 5, 1860 the Herbert's all joined the service of the Confederacy. In 1862 the CSA took over the Harbert store building and used it as a Quartermaster

William began to freight cotton to Mexico, where he sold it to the British for gold and goods. It is not known how many times William and his slaves made the long trip on "The Cotton Road". Cotton was selling for $1.25 a pound. On his last trip in the spring of 1865 at the age of 70, he sold his last wagon train of cotton and was in

Brownsville when the Federal troops occupied the town. William was arrested, and an effort was made to force him to turn over his gold to them. In case something like this might happen, he had instructed his loyal slaves to melt the grease in the grease bucket which hung beneath the rear axle of a wagon, pour it into another bucket, and then put the coins into the empty bucket and pour over the melted grease to harden on top of them As a result, the gold was never found. However William remained in custody of the Federal troops, who in their frustration over not being able to get the money, made the old man, according to the returning slaves, sweep the streets of Brownsville, Texas, as a result he died of a "broken heart" on June 21, 1865. The slaves buried his body near Brownsville and returned home with the wagon train and the gold, which was given to remaining members of the family. After his sons returned from the War, some of them with several slaves went back down to Brownsville, dug up his body and brought it back for burial in the Old City Cemetery in Columbus where you will find a large marker standing today. In the flood of 1869, William's body was one of those that washed up, and it was never recovered. My father used to say that William was buried three times (including the midnight burial in Denmark, TN) and had never found a permanent grave!

The Reid's built a new house on the Denmark/ Huntersville Road around 1854, that house is also still standing. The Meriwether's had a salon in Denmark, and a hotel at Estonallie.

Billy King

The Reid House and Family

Joab Wilson

Joab Wilson's will had been proven but not minuted in October 1846. On January 3, 1847, Thomas H. Newborn, executor, submitted an inventory and account of the recent sale of personal property. The actual will was missing. Major Joab Wilson was one of the best-known residents of West Tennessee as he helped to establish a major turnpike called the Estonallie Road that ran through Madison and Haywood counties to parts further west. He and his family were in residence in southwest Madison County by late 1828.

Major Wilson was an active Methodist layman. In May 1842, he gave that denomination a parcel of land in Denmark for the site for a meeting house. The Churches in our area were called Southern, Methodist Episcopal (Madison Deed Book 9, page 10). We know of three, Hayes Chapel, Andrews Chapel, and Denmark. Years earlier, in April 1833, he had sold a large lot out of his home tract in Denmark to the village's Presbyterian Church. (Deed Book 4, page 319.) (*The minister at that time may have been Murdoch McMIllian, he represented the Church in the Synod in 1834.*)

In 1832, Major Wilson relocated his family eight miles to the southwest to Estonallie on the Big Hatchie River in Haywood County. They lived there for years. His first wife, Mary , the mother of his children, died January 5, 1845 in the 48th year of her age. Her body was buried on their former home place in Denmark (Nashville Christian Advocate, January 31, 1845.) At the Big Black Cemetery in Denmark. They had lived in a house across the street from the cemetery. Mr. Stephen Carter had bought that house from Major Wilson. Major Wilson and his son are buried there also.

Major Wilson remarried, in August 1846, to Elizabeth H. Fitzgerald. On August 4, that year they had signed a prenuptial contract whereby John R. Watkins would hold in trust her farm in Haywood County, several slaves (some of whom still lived in Halifax County Virginia,) and personal property; it was kept together for her benefit and Major Wilson made no claim on her property. (Haywood County Deed Book M, pages 107-1090;) acknowledged August 25, 1846; this agreement was filed by the county court clerk on the morning of Major Wilson's demise, October 1, 1846.)

Stage fare from Jackson to Denmark was $1.25 in 1855

Early Baptist History in Area

May 27, 1823, Josiah W. Fort, Elder Hiram Casey, Starke Dupuy, and Obadiah Dodson met "under a grove of trees," on Fort's home place and organized The Big Black Creek Baptist Church . One religious institution, the annual CAMPGROUND MEETING, provided an opportunity for many of the people to gather together out of their usual, relative isolation on farms and plantations, "eager for human companionship" and a sociable way of worshipping their Christian deity.

After their crops of cotton and Indian corn had been planted and cultivated by late summer-time, there was a lull in tending the plants, allowing them to grow and mature before the fall harvest. The crops being thus "laid by," many families attended the closest or most interesting campground meeting.

In Madison County it was the Methodist, Cumberland Presbyterians and Baptist that organized the early religious revivals called campground meetings. Preachers would organize a schedule of preaching for a period of several days and the lay folk arrived in a locality set aside for them, convenient to a spring. They "pitched their tents and worshipped the God who made them an rejoiced together as brethren and sisters who loved the Lord that had placed them in a new and prosperous country."

The families made their "camps," temporary shelters of their wagons, cloth tents or simple cabins, having brought "bedding provisions and table wear, cooking utensils to feed and sleep all the visitors they possibly could free of charge. /Often/ Pallets were spread on the floor, one room for the women and one for the men. The cooking was done out of doors under improvised sheds. The meals were served in long sheds where a long table and benches were placed. The preaching was held under an immense brush arbor, covered over with branches from green trees /or bushes/, making it shady and cool. Long mourner's bench in front of the platform where those seeking religion and asking for prayers would kneel. Lights for the night services were provided by tall stands whereon bonfires were built on the outside, near enough to illumine the whole place brightly. The singing was 'usually/ without instruments of any kind."

Just a mile south of Denmark, a thriving village amid a prosperous farming community, about thirteen miles southwest from Jackson in Madison County, flowed the Big Black Creek, with its numerous branches, Denmark was located at an elevation of 450 feet above sea level but the land slopped southwards from the village to an elevation of 360 feet in the creek bottoms.

About two hundred and fifty feet to the west of the Bolivar road (now State Hwy. 223) that lead from Denmark to Bolivar in Hardeman County was a low place where a constantly-flowing spring lay. From the springs, on southwards, there was a gentle sloping field where the early Baptists of the area established the campground and church called by the name of Big Black Creek.

It seems likely that the Denmark area Baptists had already built a meeting house. Near the spring in the Big Black Creek bottoms. Inferentially, Washington Eddins donated "eight and a half acres, four and a half...so as to include the spring and camps: also four acres joining the said four and a half /acres/ for the Baptist Meetinghouse.

Obediah Dotson (January 5, 1793-August 4, 1854) a native Virginia, served faithfully for years as principal pastor of the Big Black congregation. Membership peaked at 240 members in 1848. In 1909 a cyclone destroyed the Church building….in the minutes books, Thomas H. Bond, church clerk, wrote, :The Presbyterians kindly gave us the use of their church until we could rebuild and get in ours. "the new building was completed in 1910. Stephen A. Carter, Church clerk, made a last entry in the church record book, October 25, 1914.

The Historic Denmark Baptist Campground and Church,, (Madison County, Tenn.) Jonathan K.. T. Smith

It is not certain where the first church building was. We know that when the cyclone hit in 1909 it was on the Big Hill and was rebuilt at this site. While it was being rebuilt they met in the Denmark Presbyterian Church.

Mar. 1826 Clover Creek Baptist Church was organized by Obadiah Dodson. It was constituted Saturday proceeding the third Lord's day. Clover Creek Church is in Medon, Tn. The original site of the church is just outside of Medon where the old cemetery is located just off Hwy. 18.

In 1826 Obediah organized the Brown Creek Baptist Church at the site where the Woodland Cemetery is now. This church split,, into Browns Creek Missionary Baptist, and Browns Creek Primitive, over sending missionaries and church music. Part of the congregation along with all the slaves formed the second church with Obediah Dodson as pastor. After the Civil War they split, again, forming the Browns Creek Missionary Baptist (White,) later changing the name to Woodland Baptist in 1870. The black congregation is still Browns Creek Missionary Baptist.

In 1826 a camp ground was organized on the Big Black Creek just out of Denmark. Many churches used the camp ground for meetings and revivals. They would last for weeks with preaching in the morning, at noon and night. You would bring your whole family even your slaves to these meetings. James Alston had suggested to Obediah that a camp ground be built. He did not want religion, it would mean he would have to sell his race horse, "Gray Eagle." He finally gave up the horse and began the entirely new race—the one to heaven. The story is that he gave the silver he got from the sale of the horse to Denmark Presbyterian and it is cast in the church bell.

In 1826, The Big Hatchie Baptist Association organized Big Black Creek Baptist Church, Obediah Dodson was appointed to oversee the receiving of churches into the association. All of West Tennessee was in the association. On September 1, 1827 the

Associational Meeting was held at the Big Black Creek Baptist Church with 31 congregations having been represented. It met again on May 15, 1828 at the Big Black Creek Church, and there were 15 churches represented . The association was beset by division with troubles over Mason's missions, "two seed," and Campbellism. The Baptist did not believe in the Masons.

Around 1836 a Quaker named Mr. J. T. Fuller was living on a plantation just about five miles from Denmark. Obediah converted him to Baptist. He told Obediah he would give him five acres of land and $500 if he would start a church closer to him. They started the Maple Springs Baptist Church, one of Fuller's requests was that a slave balcony be built in the church and it was. His slaves were all members of the church. About 1837 Obediah helped organize the First Baptist Church, Jackson, TN.

In 1842 Obediah Dodson preached the opening annual association introductory message of the Big Hatchie Association in Germantown, Shelby County, Tennessee, it is believed that Obediah was present when the Southern Baptist Convention was organized. He moved to Texas and started churches and also helped organize the Louisiana Baptist Convention becoming it first appointed missionary.

In 1870 the Browns Creek white congregation changed its name to Woodland; the black congregation remained Browns Creek Missionary Baptist, it is still a very active congregation today, the cemetery there has a few white church members buried there. .

On the fourth Saturday of September, One Thousand eight hundred and fiftieth year of our Lord, fifty-two member of Denmark Baptist Church, (Big Black Creek,) Denmark, Tennessee, having determined to constitute for themselves an independent church to be located in Cypress Creek, Madison County, Tennessee, at the suggestion of the mother church, applied for letters that they might go into such an organization. Their request was granted.

On Monday after the fifth Sabbath in September, 1850 the body preceded in the organization of Ararat Baptist Church, also referred to the Church of Christ at Ararat, adopting rules of decorum, Articles of Faith, and a Church Covenant, copies of which were recorded by Bro. William Crutchfield, church clerk, in the first volume of church records October, 1850, pages one to eight. There were fifty two who applied to the mother Church at Denmark. Now the Ararat Baptist Church in Huntersville,

Tennessee.

In 1829 a young boy wanting to go to school but with no money was offered a job on a farm in Denmark in exchange for tuition to the Denmark Male Academy. His name was Tarleton Perry Crawford. The farm was owned by Peter Smith Gayle. He lived with the Gayle's. Obediah Dodson had ordained Peter who was a member of the Big Black Creek Baptist Church in Denmark. Crawford graduated with top honors from the Academy and wanted to attend Union University which was in middle Tennessee at the time. Several of the women of the local churches decided to pay his way to Union. They were Woodland, Maple Spring, Denmark Baptist and more. The women would save the eggs laid on Sunday and the Sunday milk from their cows, and sell it and pay his tuition to Union. He graduated top of his class at Union, married, then came back to Denmark to spend several months to visit all the churches that had supported him. He left for China to be a missionary. Obediah had baptized him and ordained him. He and his wife became Missionaries to China, he wrote a book, *"Fifty Years in China."* Peter Gayle Smith became a pastor also and later and pastored many churches. Obediah had a passion for missions and he must have had a great influence on Tarleton. Peter Gayle Smith was also ordained a minister and became the first pastor of Russell Springs Baptist, now Brownsville Baptist, from there he became the pastor of First Baptist in Memphis.

In October 1909 a Cyclone hit Denmark and destroyed the Baptist and Methodist Churches, both rebuilt this was taken from the minutes of Big Black Creek Baptist Church dated Fourth Sunday in September 1910. Minutes of Big Black Creek Baptist, " On the 14th day of Oct. 1909 a severe cyclone visited Denmark destroying almost the entire town. The Baptist and Methodist Churches were completely demolished. The Presbyterians kindly gave us the use of their Church until we could rebuild and get back in ours."

"On the fourth Sunday in Sept. 1910 after a hard struggle we were able to hold our first services in our new house of worship. With preaching by our Pastor Rev. A. M. Nicholson. On which occasion our protracted meeting began. On the following Monday night, Bro. W. C. Ward came to the assistance of Bro. Nicholson. Bro. Ward did the preaching which God abundantly blessed in the salvation of souls, and in causing many backsliders to return and take up their Christian duties in the Church, and Christian were revived and made to rejoice in a Savior's love. There were 22 conversions; there were 8

Tarleton Perry Crawford

Tarlton as a young man wanted to get a education, but his finances were very bad. Peter Smith Gayle heard of his efforts and invited Crawford to come to Denmark, Tn., and live and work on his farm in exchange for his tuition at the Denmark Male Academy. He graduated top of his class and in 1848 he went to Union University which was in Murfreesboro, Tn. At the time. Several of the community church women societies help pay his cost by saving and selling the eggs and milk collected on Sundays. He graduated top of his class. March 12, 1851, he married Mrs Martha Foster. The Crawford's gave their lives in mission work in China and the church ladies from Big Black Creek Baptist, Maple Springs Baptist, Browns Creek Baptist (Woodland), Liberty Grove Baptist and Ararat Baptist helped with his living expense in China. When the Southern Baptist Mission Board was organized they sent the Crawford's a young helper, it was the famous Baptist missionary Lottie Moon. Dr. Crawford wrote a book, *"Fifty Years In China."*

additions to the Church by baptism and 1 by restoration."
T. H. Bond, Church Clerk/moderator

SOME OF THE EARLY MEMBERS OF BIG BLACK CREEK BAPTIST CHURCH

Mrs. Etta Aldrege	Mrs. Cornelia Moore
Miss Juanita Burton	Mrs. Jno. Burgess
J. L. Burton	Thomas Bond
Mrs. .Caroline Day	Mrs. Rosa Harrie
Lem Harris	R. D. McKissack
Billie McKissack	Miss Josi Rosser
Miss Sallie Weatherly	W. W. Weatherly
Mrs. H. L. Neville	Mrs Fannie Hayden
Miss Nannie Hayden	Miss Eunice Hayden
Miss Sallie Tom Reid	Miss Lillian Reid
H. H. Reid	Miss Lucile Carter
Miss Pansy Barnes	Miss Flossie Barnes

EARLY METHODIST

Major Joab Wilson was a active Methodist layman, in 1842 he gave that denomination a parcel of land in Denmark for a site of a meetinghouse of this church. (Madison County Deed Book 9, page 10) Years earlier, in April 1833, he had sold a large lot out of his home tract in Denmark to the village's Presbyterian Church. (Deed Book 4, page 319)

The Methodist Cemetery is located beside where the Church was. The earliest burial there is Sarah T. Tarver who died in 1854 and the last was William C. Colburn January 19, 1931. The oldest person buried there was Francis Meriwethe. Who was born November 7, 1774.

There are no records of the Methodist Church in Denmark, we know the location, there is a small cemetery at the site that now belongs to Big Black Creek Historical. It was a Southern Methodist Episcopal. There were two more in the area, Hayes Chapel and Andrews Chapel. Hayes Chapel was located on Hwy. 138 and there is a cemetery there. Andrews Chapel is in Huntersville and is still active, it now belongs to First Methodist in Jackson, Tn.

During the Civil War the 30th along with other companies would camp on its banks near Denmark, it provided fresh water for the animals. Estonallie played a major role during the War and Big Black Creek entered the river there. Flat boats could come up the Big Black to Denmark. "Hatchie" in the Chickasaw language means "river." Estonallie means here we cross. The Estoallie Trail comes from North Carolina, goes thru Denmark crossing the Hatchie at Estonallie, then on to the Mississippi. It was one of the first stage coach routes in West Tennessee. The first Post Office in West Tennessee was the Denmark Post Office, 1820. Steam boats were coming up the Hatchie, and then flat boats would bring the supplies to the stores in Denmark and later even into Jackson. The creek also became a major route to ship cotton to Estonallie to sell to the cotton buyers from Memphis, New Orleans, and St Louis. Cotton from the Big Black Creek Community was bringing four to five cents a pound more than cotton from any other place in the South.

In 1874 there were rumors of a railroad building this way, This was the Tennessee Midland now the N. C. and St. L. It surveyed a line through the town of Denmark,

Robert Hardee Grocery Store
Denmark Post Office 1820

through the center room of the Male Academy. It asked $3,000 of the citizens to help it bore its way through the hills. After some debate this was refused. The railroad would have to come through the town regardless. It was impossible to lay a road bed through the swamp of Big Black Creek. This was the first death knell of Denmark. The tracks bypassed Denmark causing the establishment of Mercer, Tennessee.

Early Post Offices of the area

Date Opened	Town/Community	Date Closed
1820	Denmark	Still open
1820	Forked Deer Post Office	
1824	(Later became Jackson, opened again 1824)	
1821	Oakland	1837
1824	Jackson	Still open
1824	Spring Creek	Still open
1825	Point Centre	1830
1826	Cotton Grove	1866
1827	Mount Pinson	1866
1827	Clover Creek	1836

1828	Whiting	1830
1830	Birdsong' Bluff	1833
1831	Laurel Hill	1839
1833	Annsvile	1834
1835	Health Seat	1835
1836	Medon	Still open

These are a few of the earliest.

James E. Carter received a letter dated April 6, 1905 appointing him a Rural Carrier for the Denmark Post office, he was to start May 1, 1905 at an annual salary of $666. Charles E. Harris was appointed as his substitute. Stephen Carter was appointed February 14, 1913. The route was 26 1/8 miles and the salary was $1100, Steven served for 35 years. He had started out with a horse and buggy. *(today the route is 90 miles)*

The early post office in Denmark was in the Meriweather Tavern, a stage stop. It moved to the J. F. Williamson Store when he became postmaster. It eventually was moved to Robert Hardee's store and Miss. Fanny Louise Tyson was postmaster. Mrs. Jessye L. Williamson, (Mr. Stevie Carter's sister) served from

February 27, 1917 to April 29, 1947, 30 years being the longest term of any postmaster.

* * *

The Carter Family in Denmark, Tennessee

"Eliza Rosser Carter was born in Chatham Country, North Carolina in 1827, she married Stephen Carter when she was 16 and he was 19. In 1845 they moved to West Tennessee in an overland wagon settling in Medon in Madison County. It was a long trip but lightened by the championship of others from the old state who had become restless with the desire to try their fortune in Tennessee.

Stephen had learned the tanner's trade from his oldest brother, Billy in North Carolina so he established a small tannery and did reasonably well, along with working a small farm we had acquired and also carpentry.

We remained in Medon almost 10 years. We buried three babies in the Clover Creek Baptist Cemetery just out of Medon.

In 1855 we acquired property, 54 acres, in Denmark, Tennessee with excellent advantages for a fine tannery. This was at the foot of this hill where a sand branch runs.

(just below the Denmark Presbyterian Church.) Some water was necessary for the processing of raw material into leather.

The community was in a prosperous condition with and increasing demand for good leather and manufactured articles, harnesses, saddles, bridles, boots and shoes. In a few years ith seven building, two large sheds and 25 or more good workmen, the business prospered.

The Civil War however was undoing all over the South the prospects of many good and industrious people. Denmark was occupied at different times by bot Confederate and Federal Forces.

In the latter part of the war a detachment of Cavalry in passing halted in front of the tan yard and the command was given to light the fire which burned to the ground the entire operation. It was a total loss. Many years of struggle and hard work followed. We along with many others suffered the loss of property.

Of eleven children, six survived to adulthood, one son and five daughters. Our daughter Rosa married Cyrus Harris from Galloway and reared her family here in Denmark. Out son Jim married Louise Harris, a sister to Cyrus, and they stayed with us in the old home place.

They had four children, one son and four daughters. We farmed our acres and Jim became one of the early mail carriers out of the Denmark Post Office.

Stephen was known for his exceptional memory. Our son, Jim had a beautiful bass singing voice. Our daughter Rosa wrote beautiful poetry. Our daughter Rosser loved to travel and wrote articles for the newspaper. We went back to North Carolina to visit a few remaining relatives."

Though we did not live to see it, our grandson, Stephen took over Jim's mail route upon Stephen's death and carried it for 30 years, while at the same time becoming and extensive land owner and an excellent cotton grower. (Mr. Steve as he was known always said, "I don't want any land except that which borders me." He became one of the largest land owners in Madison County, Tennessee.

A granddaughter Jessie Lynn, became Post Mistress and held that position for 30 years, the longest term served in that post office.

Written by Mrs. Louise Stevens

By FONVILLE NEVILLE –1944..

FONVILLE NEVILLE – 1944

There was a time, but long ago when the Old Big Hill lifted an oak covered head in a majestic posture to the sky.

Returning from wherever we had wandered. Its tree helmeted crest breaking the sky-line, a bastion on the wall of heaven. It had a call for us; however young and carefree or aged and weary, the heart leaped, for at its foot was home.

Perhaps it called to the first settler in such tones of verdant splendor that he said, "In its shadow I will dwell. I can raise my eyes to it for strength, ascend its slope to feel Heaven neared, and far though I range, its summit will guide me home."

He who first set foot on it had long been dust; the children who with their grandsires ascend to its crest on Sunday pilgrimages have aged and grown gray; the village whose birth it witnessed and which it had sheltered down the years, is by the wash of Time on the shores of the

Past, yet it remains as eternal as the stars.

Storms will never shake it; the blight of Time and Death will bring no dissolution to it. Long after our children's children will have lifted their eyes to it and passed in it will endure.

It is this permanence, this sense of everlasting, a rock that trembles not, which had drawn our eyes and hearts to it and find such gods as our lives require.

Relatives and friends depart; the tide of Fortune rises and falls, creeds, dogmas, philosophies thunder in our ears, the human race wanders aimlessly on. Out of the discord, the mists we raise our eyes to it and find it breasting all change, old Time, with as high a head as ever and we anchor our hopes to it and again turn to Life. It has been all things to us...a refuge, a trysting place, a hermitage, a temple, a castle, a college, a church.

At no hour was its hoary head disenchanting. From it to watch the day break from its prism of night was a scene so grand it wrung the soul with pain. One was lifted out of flesh to stand there and watch the stars come out; to lose oneself in that star dusted vault was to seat oneself at the very feet of God. And you could send your soul tracking down Heaven's Broadway, the Milky Way, to the ends of the words.

What an amphitheater one looked across facing the orange red disk of the sun wheeling its way into a purple sea beyond the run of the world! A spectacle there to make one envied of kings. Then to be a silent witness to the trailing garments of night as they swept slowly over the landscape, breaking against the old hill and drifting past to darken the while world but you. Your soul speaks of itself, the words of the old Psalmist...

"When I consider the heavens, the work of

Thy fingers, the moon and the stars which

Thou has ordained what we man that Thou are mindful of him?"

To you raise the muted sounds of a village preparing for the night...the queries tones of a belated doer of chores, the blows of an axe, he lowing of a cow, the bawling of her calf; a negro's voice raising from a croon to a barbaric chant, as his simple soul opens to the mystery of the night. A dog barks. Then silence.

A sudden rosy flush appears in the east, a golden horn of light breaks the dark purple of the earth's rim. The wind is still. A hush falls upon the world as that of an audience waiting breathlessly for the curtain to rise upon a great drama.

The tip of golden light becomes a crescent, a quarter, a half, and the great golden disk of the moon swims clear of the earth and mounts into the sky. The queen of night takes her throne and her silvery garments lace the drabness of the weary old world with splendor!

The wind was never idle on the crest of the old hill...played in all moods among the branches of the oaks. The sky was bluer. Even the clouds when angry possessed a certain dark grandeur which conquered fear. The sunlight was brighter, soul clarifying, and where it fell cloud dappled upon fields below seemed top scathed with diamond dust.

For miles on every side, the secret of the world was ours. Beneath a smudge which stained the sky was a mart of industry; there where gleamed a shield of white was a blur of a kindred village. To every point of the compass within the darkened rim of the horizon we could turn and bring to view the homes, prosperous and cultured, which made the old village a onetime Utopia of a happy land.

But the old hill's hoary head no longer lifts proudly as of old, nor calls in gallant tones to the wandered. It has no leafy crown to rise in pride against the rim of the sky. Not one tree of all the fine old oaks which rendered in a temple for our gods now stands upon its slope.

Although still garlanded with memories, a bastion still of hope, a shabbiness has come upon it. As the ages that walk erect, it yet as high lifts to the stars. The sky is as blue as ever; the distant reaches of the world just as enchanting as before. But there is no longer a song to the wind, no Aeolian harp for it to play. The sun strikes with an edge, not benedictional as of yore; there are no cloistered retreats and leafy arches for a trysting place or temple. Memory turns grey as ghosts and clutch at the hopes we carry there to renew.

As we gaze upon the old hill from a haze hung distance though our pulse quickens, for it yet signalizes home, our hearts weep for the verdant glory which once it had but has no more.

Mr. Fonville is writing about what is still called the Big Hill, at one time this is where the Big Black Creek Baptist Church was. It is one of the highest points in West Tennessee. There is a geological marker at its point. It was one of the earliest Baptist Churches in West Tennessee, founded by Obediah Dodson in the early 1820's. It could seat over 200 hundred. The slaves were also members of this Church. It is where the West Tennessee Baptist Association was formed and was the *mother Church of many of our local Baptist Churches. Maple Spring Baptist, (Mr. Fuller, a Quaker, gave Obediah Dodson five acres of land and $500 to build a Church,) Browns Creek (Woodland,) Harmony, Russell Springs, (Brownsville Baptist,) Liberty Grove, Ararat (1850,) Cane Creek and many more, out of these came many mission churches, Mercer Baptist is a mission of Maple Springs. In 1909 a cyclone (tornado) destroyed the building of Big Black Creek Baptist. It destroyed the Methodist Church also, which was across the road from Big Black Creek Baptist. The old Denmark Methodist Cemetery is still at this site and is owned by Big Black Creek Historical. The Presbyterians loaned their building to the Baptist and Methodist and all three congregations used the same building until the Methodist and Baptist could be rebuilt. Probably almost two years. Two of Big Black Baptist pastors the Day Brothers founders of First Baptist, Jackson, are buried in the Big Black Creek Cemetery in Denmark.*

* * *

Early history of the Denmark Presbyterian Church was lost, our records pick up in 1868, so we know very little about what took place before that date. We know when the church was probably organized in 1823 with a merger with the Hope Well Presbyterian. We have bits and pieces of its history. We know the first building was the school house and used by the Baptist and Methodist. The Presbyterians built the first actual building, it was a log structure next to the now cemetery. There was a second building some place. Joab Wilson gave the land for the present building. It was finished in 1854 and probably took as much as five years to build. It was constructed mostly of yellow popular. They would cut the wood in the winter when the sap was down and laid it out to dry before using it. Everything was done by hand, even the square nails that were used; they were made on site with a nail cutter. They did not know how to make a point on a nail or screw until 1853. A black smith probably stayed on the site most of the time making the thousands of nails used. The lumber was hand hewn from the logs; some are very large timbers weighting thousands of pounds. It is hard for us to imagine how they erected them all by hand. The glass for the windows was ordered and windows constructed on site, and the crate the glass came in was saved and exists today. There are no nails in the windows.

The building was a joint venture between the congregation and the Masons. They both appear on the original deed. The Masons organized in Denmark in 1847.

The lodge is upstairs over the Church. There is a pit from the ground floor to the second and is a part of the York Rite, there is only one other in Tennessee in the Episcopal Church in Franklin, Tennessee. A piece of clapboard in the top of the building has a name on it, Danny Michael, 1854.

We got an inquiry about a possible former pastor. The Bethesda Presbyterian Church in Aberdeen, N. C. will soon celebrate its 225th anniversary and wanted to know if we had any info on Murdoch McMillan . Since we did not have any records before 1868, we did not know former pastors. During research on McMillian we discovered that indeed he probably had been a pastor as early as 1834. He represented the Denmark Presbyterian Church at the Synod meeting in 1834. He moved to Western District of Tennessee, Denmark, Madison County in 1830. He was licensed to preach 3-27-1808 in the Presbytery of Orange, Buffalo Church. He was fluent in English and Gaelic, which he preached at the Buffalo Church. Doing more research we found that he had been at the Old Bluff Presbyterian Church in Wade N.C. That Church building is almost exactly like the Denmark Church . That Church was organized October 18, 1758. The story is that McMillian was born aboard ship when his parents were coming to America from Scotland in

1776. He worked at Barbecue Church in 1801 and Bethesda, Union, and Buffalo churches in 1804. He is said to have preached the first Presbyterian sermon on the banks of the Chickasaw Bluffs in what is now Memphis. His father-in-law, John Ramsey, had gotten a 5,000 acre land grant on the river, paying 5 cents an acre McMillian's sister-in-law had married Phillip Alston, they are buried in the Alston/Johnston Cemetery in Denmark. From this it is obvious that they had a strong connection to Denmark, he and his wife were teachers and could have taught at one of the Denmark Academies. They did move to Memphis where he continued to teach and establish churches.

Murdoch and his wife Jane are buried in the Trigg/McMillian Cemetery in Memphis on Trigg Ave.

He has a descendant who is a member of the Bethesda Presbyterian Church in Aberdeen, N.C. She is Mrs. Martha McLeod (Calin,) he is her fifth generation grandparent.

* * *

September 8, 1854 from the Jackson Whig

DENMARK is a rural village romantically located in Madison County about 12 miles from Jackson, Tenn. It is surrounded by a dense, industrious, wealthy, intelligent and pious population, mostly decendants of Scotch-Irish Presbyterians from North Carolina. For the past year they have had a college there where their daughters could finish their education surrounded with home influences under teachers chosen from among themselves. There are 80 students in the various classes. The course of study includes Latin, Greek, music, mathematics, Bible and all the courses necessary to a finished education. The Presbytery of the Western District should be proud of this college.

* * *

This article **appeared in the *Sheppard's, Tennessee State Gazetteer and Shippers Guide in* 1866.**

A village of Madison County in the western part of the State French, James H. Cotton factor, etc.

Gillespie, Rev James H. Pastor Denmark Presbyterian Church.

Rev. James H. Gillespie, a devout minister and a prominent citizen of Brownsville, Tenn., was born in Blount County, Tenn., August 10, 1804. His parents were Robert and Elizabeth (Houston) Gillespie, and were natives of Virginia. Rev. James Gillespie in early life was engaged with his father in the manufacturing business. In 1825 he graduated at the East Tennessee College, located at Knoxville, Tenn., at that time. He then went to Alabama and engaged in the mercantile business, but in 1827 he entered the theological college at Princeton, N. J., and prepared himself for the university, graduating from there in 1830, and the same year was licensed to preach. In 1831 he was ordained pastor of the Presbyterian Church in Somerville, Ala. He remained there until 1838, when he moved to Franklin County, Ala., where took charge of the school and filled the pulpit of the Presbyterian Church until 1842. In 1843 he moved to Denmark, Tenn., and was pastor in the Presbyterian Church until 1868, when he was called to fill the pulpit of the Presbyterian Church at Brownsville, Tenn., remaining in charge until 1872.

Since then Mr. Gillespie has been engaged in evangelical work in various churches. He has been an ernest worker in the church, and is perhaps the oldest minister in West Tennessee. October, 1830, Mr. Gillespie married Abigail C. Ellis, daughter of Col. Samuel and Priscilla Ellis, of New Jersey. They had three sons and two daughters: Mary, William F. (a minster in Texas), James E. Robert A (deceased: he was also a minister) and Martha L. James was wounded in the Battle of Franklin and died as a result of his wounds, and is buried in the Denmark Cemetery, his sister Mary is there also. *My Genealogy Hound, The History of Haywood County Tennessee.*

Hutchinson, Wm. Dealer in dry goods, boots, shoes, hats, cps, clothing, notions, groceries, furnishing goods, millinery goods, etc.

Jett, Mrs. Harriet, proprietress of boarding house.

McHenry, Wm. Proprietor woolens mill

Merriwether, WM. P. Attorney at Law

Neeley, M. S. Physician and surgeon

Newborn, Thos. H. Physician and surgeon

Dr. Newborn is buried in the Denmark Methodist

Cemetery.

Snipes, F. B. Justice of Peace

Mr. Snipes is buried in Riverside Cemetery in Jackson.

Tyson, J. A. Physician and surgeon

Dr. Tyson is buried in the Denmark Methodist Cemetery

Dr. Samuel W. Vaughan, having permanently located himself in Denmark, respectfully renders his services to the public in each department of his profession. His office will be kept at the Compting Room of S. T. & William Sanders. December 27, 1828.

* * *

DENMARK

A town of three hundred and fifty inhabitants, is situated near the western limit of Madison County, twelve miles from Jackson and sixteen miles from Brownsville, Tenn. It was incorporated in 1830. Denmark has one Female Institute, in a thriving condition, located on an elevation and commanding a full view of the town. One Masonic Lodge, numbered 154, and three churches—one Presbyterian, one Baptist, one Methodist. The people are enthusiastic over two proposed railroad lines, and manifest a stability in their enthusiasm by expressing a willingness to vote $35,000 aid. Considering the unusual excellence of the lands about the town, conceded to be some of the best in the county and its location, Denmark had the advantages of shipping that one railroad in reality, and channel into the world soon grow into a town of considerable magnitude and importance. And if her people desire to see her ranked among the growing towns of the State, they must persevere in their endeavors until at last the proposed road to Jackson becomes a road in reality, and a channel into the world of commerce for the exportation of their products and a compensating return of the world's goods and riches. Isolated as she is, she can never become a town. Connected with Jackson or any neighboring city, by a good railroad, her future as a thriving town is absolutely certain. The present days are days of progression. Wagons and carts can no long be the connecting mediums of cities of enterprise. Rivers, with their fleeting palaces, are being forgotten and ignored as revenue of transit too slow for the age, and to the iron horse with his with omnipotence and wondrous speed do the people of the day resort in their haste to transfer and sell goods from town to town. Let Denmark appreciate this truth and never rest until she has a railroad.

In the year of 1860 a most disastrous fire broke out in Denmark and swept away seventeen houses in the business part of the town. In 1866 three stores were burned and their contents lost. During the late war a battle of considerable moment was fought four miles southeast of the place at a point called Britton Lane, in which four thousand troops were engaged.

* * *

EARLY DENMARK PRESBYTERIANS

A Book of Remembrance of Denmark Presbyterian Church

Complied by Mrs. Jennie Bryan, 1934

Noted by Billy King, Big Black Creek Historical 2013

A old old church is ours
Built long ago by hearts and hands and prayers
Of those who loved God much
And built this church that they might meet with Him.

So we who use this church today
Can never think of it as just four walls
As windows, aisles and pews
Carter, Stephen, tanners,
 and dealer in hides and leather

Clayton & Roland, dealers
in dry goods, groceries, clothing, hats, caps, boots,
furnishing goods, notions, etc.

Ducker, C. B. dealer in furniture, undertaker.

Duncan, C. A. dealer in dry goods, boots, shoes, hats,
caps, clothing, notions, millinery goods, groceries, etc.

Duke, W. H. carriages and wagon maker.

Because for us ever round it clings
The memory of the hearts and hands and prayers
That built it here for God

Remembering this as week by week
Within this church we meet and talk with God
We reverent walk and lift our thoughts on high
In praise to God
Who unto us hath given His gift—this Church.

The history of the Denmark Church reaches back
more than a century. Its original organization was literally
the planting of a church in the wilderness. In the year
1824 John Wharton came with his family from Guilford,

North Carolina. He settled in the western part of Madison County, Tennessee. It was then a tangled forest whose ancient silence had never been broken by hymns of praise to God. "The oldest inhabitant who was here at that time affirms that there was not church building of any denomination near here". (Quote from an old record of the 1879"s)

Population was sparse for some time, but one by one, new settlers were coming in from the older states and from Middle Tennessee. About this time Robert Johnston, originally a native of Virginia, came from Middle Tennessee and bought a large tract of land lying up and down and near to the streams which since that day has been known as Johnston's Creek. There two good men brought with them their old fashioned religion and pretty soon began to meet for religious worship. They and their families were organized into a little church by **Rev. Daniel Weir.** They built a small log house near a little stream called Cub Creek. The membership was not more than a dozen. The church was called Hopewell. Mr. Weir lived there then in the edge of the bottom. This organization could not have been earlier than 1827. No record of exactly how long Mr. Weir preached there. His successor was **Rev Dr. Samuel Hodge** who preached at Cub Creek and at school houses and in the houses of families scattered through that part of the country.

I have not been able to find out much about Rev. Daniel Weir nor the location of the Hopewell Church, but many of the early settlers were coming from Bertie County, North Carolina and the Hopewell Synod, so I assume they named the Church from the North Carolina Hopewell Synod. Many were also from the Orange County Synod. We have found a direct connection with several Presbyterian Churches in that area, one is Bethesda Presbyterian organized by the Scots in 1790, it is located on the Old road between Southern Pines and Aberdeen, N. C. Another one is Old Bluff Presbyterian(Old Bluff looks just like Denmark Church,) in Wade, Black River, N.C. Rev. James Campbell, who was born in Campbelltown, Kintyre, Scotland about 1705, came to American about 1730. He came to North Carolina from Presbytery of Philadelphia about 1757. He commenced his preaching among the Scots of Old Bluff in both Gaelic and English, we find this also in several pastors of the Denmark Church. The Old Bluff Church building is built on the same design as the Denmark Church, it first appeared that the Denmark Congregation copied the floor plan of Old Bluff, but Old Bluff was built in 1858 and Denmark in 1854.

I find Rev. Samuel Hodge all over the place, the Denmark Church was the largest in West Tennessee when he was pastor, but I think he was one of the founders of First Presbyterian in Jackson, Tennessee. In a copy of <u>The Jackson Gazette</u> dated May 29, 1824, he is listed as performing many wedding in Jackson. I find him again organizing the First Presbyterian in Covington, Tennessee August 15th 1829. Rev. Hodge was a agent for the <u>Calvinistic Magazine</u> in July, 1830, copies were 3 cents each.

Union Church of the Presbytery of Western District, was organized by Rev. Samuel Hodge, on Thursday, September 26th, A.D. 1839. In the community were members of the Denmark and Brownsville churches, who united together to form the new organization, from which circumstance the name of Union was adopted. A session was convened at the date given above, with Rev. Mr. Hodge as moderator. Several other pastors of the Denmark Church preached at Union....Rev. Alexander Van Court, Rev. Murdoch McMillian, Rev. Dr. Elijah Slack, and Rev. J. H. Gillespie. On the 1st of April 1851, the Union Church had 150 members.

This church, Hopewell (the exact site is not known,) was about nine miles Northeast of Denmark near the Memphis to Bristol Highway. The Memphis-Nashville-Bristol Highway was Tennessee's first state road, it was built in 1911, but I am sure that it followed the old wagon trails. The good road movement begin in 1890 and the road was to cross the three grand division of the State. It was to be a 500 miles all weather road. In 1926 it became U.S. Hwy. 70.

Which is only a few miles from Denmark.

An Indian trading post had been established at what is now Denmark about 1818, possibly earlier. After the removal of the Indians to Alabama—1819—1820—a village began to rapidly grow up in the center of this fertile, high and healthful region.

(This trading post was on the Big Black Creek operated by John and William Harbert. There was also a younger brother Stephen, their mother was a Crocket, aunt of David Crocket.)

In the minutes of the Presbyterian Synod Western District, Volume 17, 1863 and the Tennessee Minutes of the General Assembly, a charter was given the Denmark Church for the Denmark Female College.

There was one other in West Tennessee it was at Shiloh. The Denmark Male

Academy was incorporated in 1843, Dr. W. L. Slack, principal.

An interesting "bit" regarding the early settlement of this village is found in a clipping from an old newspaper dated Feb. 25, 1878, The article was written by **Rev. Dr. Samuel C. Caldwell** who was the pastor of the Presbyterian Church. ***Rev. Caldwell was the highest paid minister in West Tennessee, his salary was $1,200 a year.***.

"There are in the United States exactly a dozen towns by the name of Denmark. But the most important, perhaps, and the most interesting to your readers, is in the western part of Madison County, one mile from the celebrated Big Black Spring whose crystal waters have refreshed many a weary traveller. The site for a town must have been selected on account of its elevation and picturesque views. No doubt it was a commanding locality when half a century ago, our father pitched their tents here on the then heavily wooded mounts. There are two beautiful eminences, known as the "Big Hill" and "College Hill". The former is more conspicuous for altitude and can be seen for miles around. It is sometimes

RAILROAD MAN VISITING DENMARK

DENMARK STORE

STORE

ABOUT 1917

used as an observatory when the citizens wish to look down on Brownsville and Jackson. There are no buildings on this hill, but the top is decorated with a cluster of small, graceful oaks among which lovers sometimes stroll at moonlight picnics. On the summit of College Hill stands the spacious old Building in which as many ladies from all parts of the country were educated before the war. Many hallowed associations cluster around that old college and many a accomplished woman lives over again in memory the bright and joyous days of her girlhood that were spent within those walls."

A few Presbyterians had come to Denmark and a village was growing up in the center of a fertile, high healthful region. The village was located upon two circular hills. On one of these hills stood a school house used by various denominations of Christians for religious services. It was announced one Sabbath that there would be preaching in that house on the following Sabbath. Some other denomination (Baptist) then appointed a service for the same house. A few of the Presbyterians became offended and before the next Sabbath they had built a church of their own and had preaching at the appointed hour. A church was built in a week. To be sure it was not a great building but it answered the purpose for several years. This little church was called by many

"Jonah's gourd."

On the twenty-third of February 1833 there was a re-organization combining the members who had been worshipping at Cub Creek with those who had settled in or near Denmark. The services of the re-organization took place in the building which, like the heaven and the earth, was made in the space of six days. On April the fifth, 1833 **Rev. A. A. Campbell** reported the re-organization and requested that the church be known in the future as the Denmark Presbyterian Church. The request was granted by the Presbytery. After these five or six years of struggling the church began a new career of usefulness with a new name.

The latter part of this year (1833) a young licentiate, **Alex McNutt**, was teaching school in Jackson. He had been sent out by the Board of Home Missions and come to preach to the little body of Presbyterians at Denmark. He and a young man got up a camp meeting at Big Black Springs south of Denmark. **Dr. A. A. Campbell and Mr. McNutt** did the preaching and there was poured out a mighty blessing on scores and scores. The old church which was called "Jonah's Gourd," in derision was pulled down and a commodious house of worship was erected in 1834. Jonah's Gourd was a log structure, built after the dispute with the Baptist over Sunday meeting. This building was the school also, so the Jonah's Gourd building was actually the first building built for Church only.

Dr. Campbell's services were secured and he began to preach regularly in the new church. The church was gradually gaining strength by accessions from North Carolina and other states. It enjoyed the services of Dr. Campbell. The elders were John Wharton, Robert Johnston, James Alston, John Ingram and John Johnston.

John Alston is buried in the Johnston/Alston Cemetery on Denmark/Jackson Road and John Ingram is buried in the Denmark Presbyterian Cemetery along with is son Capt. John Ingram, commander of the Denmark Danes.

Rev. Murdock McMillan preached here irregularly and on special occasions. He was a great preacher and gifted in prayer, he preached the first Presbyterian sermon ever preached in what became Memphis in December 1824. He was standing on the bank of the Mississippi River at the Chickasaw Bluffs.

Murdoch McMillian was born aboard a ship when his parents were coming to America from Scotland *in 1776. (Union Church history says he was born in Robeson County, NC in 1776) Rev. Murdock McMillian was the son of John McMillian who gave the land for Raft Swamp Church, NC. He was licensed but not ordained in 1802, was a member of Orange and then Fayetteville Presbyteries. He worked at Barbecue Church in 1801, Bethesda, Union and Buffalo churches in 1804. He helped to create a classical school called Solemn Grove Academy at the head of the Rockfish Creek near Mr. Helican (now called Paint Hill in Aberdeen, NC), a few miles east of current Old Bethesda, and stayed at Bethesda until 1811. He was the only teacher at the Academy and was greatly assisted by his wife, in running the school. Tuition for the basic school classes was $2.50 per quarter. The Latin and Greek Classic education was $4.00. Room and board could be included for $15.00. (Moore Co. History**) E. T. McKeithen said that :Rev. McMillian was a minister of great force and ability and exerted a wide influence in the North Carolina Synod." Rev. McMillian then went on to create and preach in Euphronia Academy near Sanford on Sunday nights in the year 1811 and had organized the Euphronia Presbyterian Church by 1819. Rev McMillian was fluent in both English and Gaelic, so he held two services on the Sabbath, one in each* *language (with an intermission between the services.) Rev. McMillian continued his labors until the year 1830, when he moved to the Western District Presbytery in Tennessee. He preached the first Presbyterian sermon ever on the Chickasaw Bluff of the Mississippi, now Memphis, Tenn. His wife came from a prominent family in the Chatham Co. area and together the Ramsey family migrated to Tennessee. McMillian never returned to NC, living organizing churches and dying in West Tennessee in 1851. He has many descendants living in that state and throughout the Midwest. The church was known as Bethesda by this time, rather than Church at the Head of Rockfish. He is buried in the Trigg/McMillian Cemetery on East Trigg Ave.in Memphis. In 2013 he still had relatives in Bethesda, Martha MacLeod, she will be 90 in November 2013.. She still lives on the land that her ancestors purchased in 1700's All of her life she has served the Church...as kindergarten teacher, certified Christian Educator, office secretary, tour guide to Scotland, president of NC Presbyterian Son and much more.*

McMillian's father in law, John Ramsey got 5,000 acres on the Mississippi River along with John Rice who also got 5,000 acres, Rice sold his land to John Overton who established the City of Memphis. I feel that Rev. McMillian established the First Presbyterian of Memphis. While Rev. McMillian was pastor of Denmark Presbyterian they bought the land where the present building is in 1833. This is the third building of the Denmark Church. I am sure he and his wife taught in the schools. He represented the Denmark Church at the Synod in 1833.

When Rev. McMillian and his wife Jane moved to Memphis, he continued to organize Presbyterian Churches and took charge of Spring Vale Academy, he helped organize First Presbyterian in Memphis in 1826 and Second Presbyterian in 1844.

Jane McMillian sister had married Phillip Alston, the Alston's were very active members of the Denmark Presbyterian Church. In 1830 James Alston, was owner of a celebrated race horse, "Gray Eagle,:" James was a world-minded person, he met a Mr. McNutt at the Big Black Creek Campground during a camp meeting. He became a Christian. He had been racing his horse at the race track at Estonallie, he decided to give up racing, he had recently won silver at the trace, when asked what he would do with all the silver, he replied, "I don't know." But he gave all the silver for the casting of the bell at the Denmark Presbyterian Church. The bell can be heard for seven miles around Denmark.

The bell is one of the most prized possessions of the Church, it rang for as long as was surmised that it took the soldiers to march to Jackson. The bell was cast in North Carolina and is said to contain many pieces of silver donated by the ladies of the Church. It has been a part of every church service, wedding, and funeral, and has served as an excellent fire alarm. On October 14, 1979, at a special gathering, it was rung 150 times for the Sesqui-centennial Anniversary.

Rev. McMillian preached both in Gallic and English, often preaching two sermons on Sunday in each language.

Dr. Campbell's ministry closed about 1838 or 1839. He was succeeded by Rev. **Johnson E. Bright.** His connection with Denmark as stated supply was short but pleasant and edifying to the people.

In September 1840 **Rev. Alexander Van Court** was ordained and installed pastor of this church. The young man was very devoted to his calling and wherever he went he carried the sunshine of good cheer. His ministry at Denmark was short but brilliant. The church was then like a growing infant gaining strength perceptibly every day.

Rev. Van Court was pastor of Fourth Presbyterian Church, later Central Presbyterian Church in St. Louis, MO. This is where Rev. Van Court was pastor when he died, he was this Churches first pastor, the Church was greatly affected by his death. Rev. S.. J. P. Anderson was then called as Central's pastor.

Rev. Van Court spent five and a half months among the Churches of the West Tennessee Synod and also in Mississippi. He died of cholera July 1849.

When **Rev. J. H. Gillespie** came to Denmark in 1843 he found what he was wont to call "that noble band of elders". Rev. J. H. Gillespie was a strong, influential one. The membership was more than one hundred and fifty. Liberal contributions were made to foreign and domestic missions and to the board of education

Rev J. H. Gillespie's father John Gillespie was born in Guilford County, NC in March 10, 1769, his parents were Scotch Irish Presbyterians and very dedicated, their first born son was dedicated to God at his birth. The son took a full course of study under the famous educator and divine Rev. David Caldwell, D.D. The Gillespie's had come to Tennessee in 1808. John organized the Bethel Presbyterian Church in McNairy County, Tennessee, Sept. 7, 1823, he was old and full of days, he died November 4, 1834.

Rev. J.H. Gillespie *was pastor during the Civil War, he is credited of preaching a sermon standing on the porch of the Church to the Denmark Danes before they left for duty in Jackson. Rev. Gillespie chose as his scripture* <u>1st Kings XXII:34</u> *"And a certain man drew a bow at a venture and smote the King of Israel between the joints of the harness" —and preached there from what to was a tender and comforting sermon. Dr. Gillespie's son was wounded and died from his wounds. He is buried in the Denmark Church Cemetery.*

In 1847 **Rev. Gillespie** invited **Dr. Daniel Baker,** a great revivalist to Denmark. A camp meeting was held at the old Alston place half way between Jackson and Denmark. It was a gracious meeting and good permanent effects followed.

(<u>*The Jackson Newspaper*</u>*) reported that over 1,000 people attended this revival. That had to build a shed to hold all the people that were coming, it lasted for several weeks.) Dr. Daniel Baker was a Presbyterian circuit- riding minister who helped organize the first Presbytery in Texas in 1840 and Austin College in 1849.*

Rev. John Gillespie, a devote minister and prominent citizen graduated at the East Tennessee College, located at Knoxville, Tenn. He then went to Alabama and engaged in the mercantile business, but in 1827 he entered the theological college at Princeton, N.J. and prepared himself for the university, graduating from there in 1830, and the same year was licensed to preach. In 1831 he was ordained pastor of the Presbyterian Church at Somerville, Ala. He remained there until 1838 when he moved to Franklin County, Ala. where he took charge of the school and filled the pulpit of the Presbyterian Church until 1842. In 1843 he moved to Denmark, Tennessee and was pastor in the Presbyterian Church until 1868 when he was called to fill the pulpit of the Brownsville Presbyterian Church remaining until 1872. He was the oldest minister in West Tennessee. October 1830 he had married Abigail C. Ellis. They had three sons and two daughters, Mary, William F. (A minister in Texas) James E, Robert A. who was wounded in the Civil War and came home to Denmark, Tenn. where he died and is buried in the Denmark Cemetery. Dr. Gillespie is buried in Brownsville, Tenn.

He was the second president of Austin College. One of his first churches, 1822, was Second Presbyterian, Washington, D. C. where John Quincy Adams and Andrew Jackson were members. He was a very powerful speaker and evangelist. I think this speaks of the power of the Denmark Presbyterian Church to be able to have such an outstanding minister to come to Denmark.

In 1848 they bought a manse and in 1834 they sold the building to the Cumberland Presbyterians and a much large building was built and completed in 1854. A female college was built in 1850. The professor was **A. L. Lewis**. There was already a male academy here.

Several young men were called into the ministry, William J. McKnight, R. L. Neely, **William F. Gillespie**, the son of Rev. Gillespie,James H. Gillespie was also called. This young preacher responded to the call of duty in the Civil War, and he died in camp at Columbus, Kentucky, January 19, 1862. His body was brought home for burial and his remains now rest in the cemetery in Denmark.

"1860 was a time of refreshing from the presence of the Lord," There was a gracious outpouring of the Holy Spirit. Forty three members were added to the church on profession of faith within a few weeks.

In 1861 the bugle blast of war sounded and echoed among the hills of Denmark and her sons responded. Some went out and were slain on the red field of battle and some died from the fevers which hovered over the camps. In the early part of the war Denmark was over-run by the Northern army. Schools were closed. Worship was frequently interrupted , the pastor preached sermons of comfort and helped his people bear their troubles. His own boys were in the army and one had died on the tented field.

On August 31, 1862, 1500 Federal troop marched in from Estonallie Landing on the Hatchie lead by Colonel Elias S. Dennis. They camped in and around the Denmark Presbyterian Church in the Mulberry woods. They were on their way to defend Jackson against attack by General Nathan Bedford Forrest. They were the 30th, 20th, 4th Illinois Calvary and a two gun section of Battery E, 2nd Illinois Light Artillery. When they came into Denmark, they had always camped on the Church grounds. The Whig

If our old church building could speak it could tell many interesting things. It is said that **John A. Murrel** once preached from this pulpit and entertained the people while members of his gang stole their horses. Very probably this never happened. The second story of the church was used as a Masonic Hall and the women met there to sew and pray for their loved ones. The uniforms for the Denmark Danes were made on the second floor by the women of the town. *(The Masons are on the deed of the church and the upstairs is still sit up as a Masonic Hall, the Denmark Masons date to 1847)*

Capt. Gus Reid (son of "Uncle Tommie Reid) once hid under the church when pursued by Union Soldiers. Finis Bryan who was a mere boy and proud of his uniform wore it to "preaching". He was captured and taken to the prison in Chicago. Another soldier present in uniform also lay flat on the floor in one of the old-fashioned boxed in pews with doors, and lady friends standing around in hoop skirts hid him completely ,so he was not captured.

The Presbyterian Synod meets at the church, April 7, 1864.

In 1867 Rev. Gillespie was released from the pastoral care of the church, thus ending a pastorate of more than 24 years. **Rev . James Houston Gillespie** was born of Scotch-Irish parents in East Tennessee 10, 1804. He began his academic studies with Rev. Samuel Doak, D. D. one of the original and great educators of East Tennessee. Mr. Gillespie graduated from Princeton in

1830, took charge of two churches in Morgan County Alabama. There he remained eight years. The Denmark Church had 145 members, Jackson had 85.

Rev. Cyrus K. Caldwell was received from Orange Presbytery, North Carolina. He came second Sabbath in February 1865.

In the Session minutes dated March 30th, 1870:

"The object which calls us together today is one of sadness, The Rev. C. K. Caldwell our faithful and able pastor has been called to his reward. Death at all times is a hard time, but the death of a beloved Pastor is an event of deep interest that brings gloom and sorrow over many hearts. Our dear pastor hd been with us for nearly nine years, breaking into the bread of life, and by preaching and example teaching us the way of life. He has left us in sorrow, but we are sure, that our loss is his gain: and that while we remain her in tears, his is in the Church in Glory."

Rev. Samuel Caldwell came in the summer of 1876. In June 1878 he married a great-grand daughter of **Rev. Murdoch McMillian**, who often preached to the Denmark Church. In 1883 **Rev. Samuel W. Newell** was called. On one occasion he himself took the emblems of

Christ's body and blood to an old Negro, who was a devote Christian and had enjoyed the services from a "back seat" in the church but had been over looked.

We have the records of the session meeting from 1868, earlier ones were destroyed during the Civil War. They are very interesting, this is the entry Sept. 10, 1871.

Denmark, Tenn.

Sept. 10 1871

Session met at 3 p.m. and was opened with prayer, a full session being present.

Clerk of the Session was ordered to cite the following members of the Church on the 30th 2:00 p.m. to answer to the charges affixed to their names as follows,—

James S. Reid Swearing, fighting, and unchristian conduct.

John. F. Williamson Dancing and unchristian conduct

John M. Gillaspie Intoxication and unchristian conduct

John R. Alston Dancing and unchristian conduct

Session Clerk closed with prayer. J. B. Neely Clerk

None of those charged appeared on the 30th, but James S. Reid did appear Oct 28 to repent of his sins satisfactory to the session and the case was dismissed. In all the early churches the church did call its members before the body to repent or their names would be removed from the role or as they would say, "from the watch care of the Church."

Rev. Cyrus K. Caldwell was the grandson of Rev. Dr. David Caldwell D. D., he was a member of Constitutional Convention in 1776, the British camped on his plantation and burned his library and sermons. Dr. Samuel was Cyrus father...all Presbyterian ministers. Cyrus died in Jackson, Tennessee.

Dr. Samuel Criaghead Caldwell, father was also a Presbyterian Minister, at times the crowds coming to hear him were so large they had to move the services outside.

On October 14, 1909, a terrible cyclone almost devastated Denmark, entirely demolishing the Big Black Creek Baptist and the Denmark Methodist Church, un roofing and other wise injuring the Presbyterian. But thanks to God who put it into the heart of friends to help us, in less than two weeks our church was ready for services. (*This cyclone was a part of the down turn at*

Denmark, many of the homes and businesses were destroyed and not rebuilt, several people lost their lives.)

In the minute of Big Black Creek Baptist Church dated September 25, 1910,"the church on motion and vote was also tendered the members of the Presbyterian Church for use of their house of worship during our stay with them." The Baptist also help pay for cleaning the building.

Baptist and Methodist were rebuilt in the course of the next two years.

(They used the Presbyterian church until their churches could be rebuilt. In the old minutes of Big Black Baptist, they paid a weekly fee to help clean the church. Remember the story of the three churches holding services in the same log house, then Presbyterian got upset over the Baptist coming on the wrong Sunday, now we find them using the same building again.)

In a letter dated October 11, 1990, Charles D. Harvey, Executive Presbytery Stated Clerk wrote, " At the request of the four members of the Denmark Presbyterian Church, The Presbytery of Memphis dissolved the Denmark Church effective October 9, 1990."

WATCH AN OLD BUILDING WITH CARE;

GUARD IT AS BEST YOU MAY,

AND AT ANY COST FROM ANY INFLUENCE OF DILAPIDATION.

COUNT ITS STONES AS YOU WOULD THE JEWELS OF A CROWN;

SET WATCHES ABOUT IT AS IF AT THE GATES OF A BESIEGED CITY;

BIND IT TOGETHER WITH IRONS WHEN IT LOOSENS;

STAY IT WITH TIMBERS WHEN IT DECLINES.

DO THIS TENDERLY, AND REVERENTLY, AND CONTINUALLY,

AND MANY A GENERATION WILL STILL BE BORN

AND PASS AWAY BENEATH ITS SHADOW.

JOHN RUSKIN

Denmark Presbyterian Church "A House of Worship during War"

The National Register listed the church, built by slaves in 1854,played a significant role in Madison County's Civil War experiences. In April 1861, days after the firing on Ft. Sumter, 104 local men formed a company called The Denmark Danes, later part of the 6th Tennessee Infantry Regiment C. S. A. The community gathered at the church to watch the new soldiers assemble before they left for Camp Beauregard in nearby Jackson. At the ceremony Emma Cobb presented a silk flag with the company's name to Capt. John Ingram. Rev. Gillespie gave the sermon.

On the eve of the Battle of Britton's Lane on August 31, 1862, the 20th and 30th Illinois infantry Regiments commanded b y U. S. Col. Elias S. Dennis camped in a grove of mulberry trees nearby the church. After the battle, the cavalry brigade of C. S. A. Gen. Frank C. Armstrong spent the night in Denmark on their return south. The Confederates kept their prisoners on the church's second

Big Black Creek Baptist Church second building built after cyclone of 1909, Note two towers, door on the left is for men and one on the right is for women and children. Church was established in 1823 by Obediah Dodson..

floor, which was a Masonic Lodge. Inscriptions written by these Federal soldiers can still be seen along the bottoms of the walls.

By 1863, the Union army controlled much of West Tennessee. Local Confederates returning to Denmark on leave had to be careful. During one Sunday service here, a Federal patrol burst into the church and two visiting Confederates had to hide under their girlfriends' hoop skirts to avoid capture.

Nearby the church is its historic cemetery, where three Confederate veterans, probably many in unmarked graves. Capt. Ingram, commander of the Denmark Danes is buried here.

Gen. Armstrong stated, " On September 2, 1862, we captured two pieces of artillery, destroyed a portion of the wagon train, and took 213 prisoners...." This is the group held captive in the Masonic Lodge over the Denmark Presbyterian Church.. Armstrong stayed here several days, then went on to Estonallie.

It is obvious from the research that many very famous people visited the Church. When the treaty between the Chickasaw and Andrew Jackson was signed in 1818 he was in and out of the area and we know he visited some of the early congregation, we also know that family members of President James K. Polk were members of the church and many were married at the Church, there is a French/Polk Cemetery just up the road from the Church with his relatives buried there and the funerals probably were held at the Church. It is also thought that General Ulysses Grant probably came though Denmark on his way to Memphis and Holly Springs since it was on the main Stage Coach Road. If only the walls could talk, they could tell many great stories. .

* * *

Cochrane, minister and teacher, by Faye Tennyson Davidson

Bolivar-Times

David Cochran was born Feb 24, 1808 in Gorticross, a parish of Glendermont County Derry, near Londonderry, Ireland. He was educated in Old College Belfast and received a general certificate in 1828. He was licensed to preach by Letterkenny Presbytery and ordained in Ballygawley County Tyrone, Nov. 30, 1830.

He came to America about 1844, landing in New York. He came to Paducah, Ky, from there he began a teaching career. He moved to Paris, Tennessee where he married July 28, 1846. Martha Reeves Bradley.

"The Civil War Reminiscences of John Johnson"

***Tenn. Historical Quarterly*, Vol. 13 Mar. 1954 No 1**

"Old David Cochrane was then teaching school in the old Academy at Denmark. He had great reputation as an excellent teacher and for scholarly attainments, and for using the rod with a liberal hand on dull or reffactory boys. It was decided that I should attend his school which I did for a short time. Mr. Cochran was immensely fat man with very short legs, and it was curiosity to me to see him walk. Something which he did very rarely except going and coming to and from the School House.

He went to the school house very early in the morning had some scholars who recited to him before the ordinary breakfast time. And he generally remained seated at his desk from that early hour until noon, when he would sometime walk about the house, just to "stretch: his limbs as he expressed it.

He was a native Irishman, and though he had been teaching since his youth at Paris and Jackson, his brogue was very decidely Irish. While fussy and irritable he was a really fine old fellow and I soon learned to esteem him very highly. He treated me with great respect and he and I never had the slightest disagreeable thing to occur between us. He, several years before, had been ordained a minister in the Presbyterian Church and was a sincere Christian."

In the article form the Bolivar Times it mentions that Rev. David Cochrane preached April 7, 1860 at Union church. There was a Union Church built by the same plan as the Denmark Church and also a Union Cemetery, one of the earliest in the area. That building was sold to the Methodist, they tore it down and built the Union Grove Methodist Church located on U. S. Hwy 70 at a small settlement called Union. I feel sure since Rev. Cochran was ordained that he probably from time to time preached at the Denmark Church. He died during the Civil War at the age of 64

Rev. Cochran's great-great-grand-daughter Monita Carlin lives in Boliver, Tennessee

* * *

I don't know when this article was written, but would guess around 1866, it really list two of the things that caused the down fall of Denmark. The railroad plan did not go through, the town did not want the riff raff associated with railroads, not the dirty smoke. But, one of the main reasons was the Big Black Creek bottoms which the track would have to go through or around, which they did. Later they did try and put in a small gage track and there are still ruminates of it. The second thing mentioned is the fire that did destroy seventeen of the business houses. Then in 1909 a cyclone hit the town destroys many more of its buildings. The Baptist and Methodist Churches were both destroyed. They did rebuild.

MASONIC LODGE DENMARK, TENNESSEE

The Denmark Lodge dates to 1847 and operated until 1861. Few records prior to 1866 have survived. It appears on the deed of the Denmark Presbyterian Church in 1854. Major Joab Wilson gave the land for the Church and Masonic Lodge. Adolphus Britton was initiated into the lodge on September 6, 1865 and remained a member until his death May 16, 1873. He is buried in the Denmark Methodist Cemetery.

About twelve men that we know served as Worshipful Master between 1853 and 1887. T. D. Tarver, J. R. Alston, Lewis T. Williamson, T. M. Meriwether, W. A. Morgan, W. M. Henry, Thomas Bond, H. P. Hudson, W. D. Fletcher, W. D. Utley, A. R. Reid, and L. B. Campbell.

There is a pit in the front room of the Denmark Church, it is square, framed, opening on the 2nd floor, it has a handmade ladder installed before the roof was put on the Church, it is a part of the York Rite and Royal Arch Rite of the Masons. There is only one other known ladder and it is in a Church in Franklin, Tennessee.

There were 97 Union Soldiers held prisoner from the Battle of Britton land in the lodge after the Battle of Britton Lane. They were from the 30th, 17th and 20th Illinois.

* * *

Time line for events in Denmark

1818 Treaty signed with Chickasaw Indians for West Tennessee

1818 John and William Harbert established a trading post on Big Black Creek

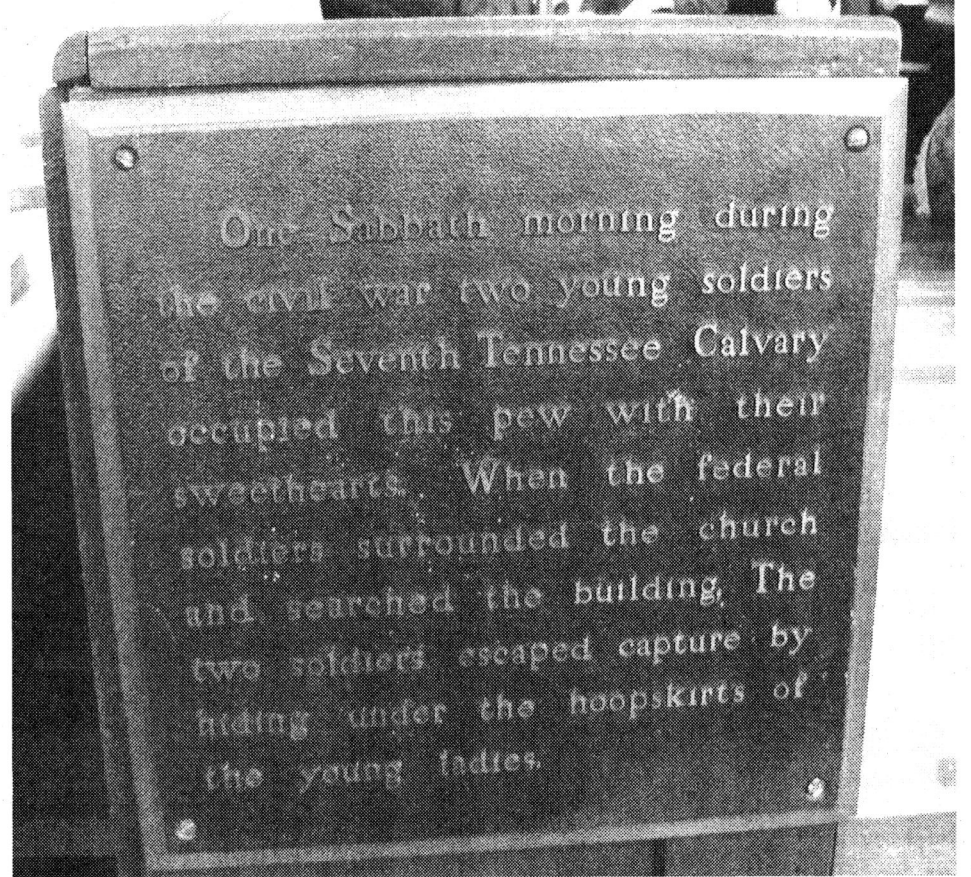

One Sabbath morning during the civil war two young soldiers of the Seventh Tennessee Calvary occupied this pew with their sweethearts. When the federal soldiers surrounded the church and searched the building, The two soldiers escaped capture by hiding under the hoopskirts of the young ladies.

1820 Denmark Post Office opened, first in West Tennessee

1821 Denmark Presbyterian Church organized at a brush arbor on Cub Creek

1821 Big Black Creek Baptist Church Organized by Obediah Dodson

1822 Denmark first settlement, John Rose was a squatter already in log house

1822 Log School House built on Big Black Creek

1823 Maple Springs Baptist organized

1826 "Red Rover" steam boat came up Hatchie to Estonallie

1827 Hopewell and Denmark Presbyterian merged

1827 Baptist Association Meeting at Big Black Creek Baptist

1828 Big Hatchie Baptist Association organized at Big Black Creek Baptist

1830 Denmark Incorporated

1831 Joab Wilson operated a ferry at Estonallie

1831 Methodist held Camp Meeting at Big Black Creek

1833 Denmark Presbyterians built first church building/ Presbyterians, Baptist and Methodist had been using the school for worship on different Sunday's

1834 Steam boat "Denmark" arrived at Estonallie, having been built for Hatchie River

1842 Methodist built new church building and established cemetery

1842 Denmark Presbyterians bought lot for new church

building, where present church is

1842 William Harbert and Mary Wadell Harbert built new house, present McKessick House in Denmark,Tn.

1846 Steam Boat "The Belle of the Hatchie" was built form travel from Memphis to Brownsville and Estonallie

1847 Denmark Masonic Lodge organized

1850 52 Members of Big Black Creek Baptist formed the Ararat Baptist Church at the suggestion of the mother Church

1850 Female Academy built

1850 Male Academy opened

1852 Construction of Reid House started for James William Reid and Nancy Temperance Reid, it took five year to build

1854 Denmark Presbyterian Church built

1854 Silver Bell at Presbyterian Church installed.

1860 17 downtown stores burnt

1861 May 5th Denmark Danes left for Camp Beauregard

1862 30th Illinois camped in Mulberry trees behind Denmark Presbyterian Church

1862 Battle at Britton's Lane

1862 Sept 1, Prisoners placed upstairs in Denmark Presbyterian Church

1866 Four store buildings burnt in downtown

1867 Fire ruined most of business district

1871 Denmark Missionary Baptist Church organized (black)

1871 Big Black Creek Baptist built new building on Big Hill

1872 Citizens raised $25,000 for a rail line to be known as the Denmark, Brownsville and Durhamville Railroad

1873 Black Methodist Church organized now CME Church

1885 High School was chartered in Denmark

1903 Three more stores burnt

1906 Three stores and post office burnt

1909 April, "Cyclone" hit Denmark, destroying Big Black Creek Baptist and Methodist Churches

1914 Big Black Creek Baptist closed at one time the largest congregation in Denmark with over 240 members not counting the slaves.

1917 Denmark High School opened

1924 12 buildings and cotton gin burned

1947 Denmark High School girls basketball team won state championship

1953 Last service in Denmark Methodist Church, May 10th

1979 150th anniversary of incorporation

1983 Denmark Presbyterian Church placed on National Register

1983 Denmark lost its city charter, became unincorporated

1990 October 9, Denmark Presbyterian Church officially closed

1991 West High School Closed

By 1970 the population had gone down to 69 from one point being at one time the largest town in West Tennessee. In order to keep a charter a town must have 25 residence.

* * *

Along Rural By-Paths (Doctor Robinson)

By FONVILLE NEVILLE

The last of Denmark's old guard is done¯Doctor Robinson.

With the passing of Doctor Robinson went the quaintest character of an old town whose history could be well told in a biography of characters such as he.

With the passing of Doctor Robinson went the quaintest character of an old town whose history could be well told in a biography of characters such as he.

With the passing of Doctor Robinson went the quaintest character of an old town whose history could be well told in a biography of characters such as he.

So long had Doctor Robinson been identified with Denmark, that the name of Denmark and Dr. Robinson had become synonymous. The association of the two could not be separated. And but for the many changes which have marred the old place¯fire and desertion beating it into the dust, leaving a ghostly and ghastly resemblance, without Doctor Robinson it would not be the same. Now inured to such passing, apathetic under the weight of years, it but marks another empty place and stands by with resignation. As to others it has pointed, so of him it will say, "His shop stood here. His house there."

Of course it is just the natural attitude of the mind, but nevertheless there is a disquieting feeling in the difference of the thought that one has gone away for a short stay and gone away forever. So Doctor Robinson's little house had that disquieting difference.

It is peculiarly lonely and set apart. No smoke rises from its chimney. In its accustomed place dances a wrath of loneliness. The door is closed with a bleak finality. No suffusing glow of expectancy, waiting or welcome mellows it's in animation with an atmosphere of tendency. Stark and cold its gate portal.

A quarter of a century ago Denmark could not have gotten along without Doctor. He was as essential to the town's wellbeing as one of the organs of the body is essential to life. As the Big Hill fell on the home comer's gaze assuring home was only a short distance, so did the presence of Doctor assure the common place functions of our daily life.

We went to him for most everything. "But religion," as he once chucklingly remarked to a Methodist preacher. A gleaner of every path and road he traversed on the premise that someday whatever thing he found would come in useful, his shop became a veritable museum of parts of most every mechanical contrivance made. There was nothing scarcely in the catalogue of mechanics but what could be found there.

To a natural aptitude he added years of training, so there was nothing the Doctor couldn't do. The anatomy of a cow differed little from the anatomy of a wagon in his conception and daring. And as for the simpler ailments flesh was heir to, he conquered them easily.

Toothache? Sure the Doctor could pull it. He had one pair of forceps, but Proteus-like they could change their form to fit any tooth. And if he ever got hold of that tooth it came! Stomach ache!- "Come in here, honey. I've got some flux weed that's the very thing. Take a glassful at bedtime and in the morning you'll be well."

He was the patron saint of all the animals. He was called on to prescribe for most every species of animal, dogs, cats, horses, cows, pigs.

As cow practitioner he earned the title of Doctor. Never a cow in a far radius was afflicted but what Doctor Robinson was called in. Of course in the old day's cows never contracted or fell victims to any other diseases but hollow tail and hollow horn. Doctor's remedies were simple but in many cases effective.

To us kids he was a source of ever revealing wonder. Good naturedly and patiently he answered every demand we made upon him. He fashioned our baseball bats, fixed our spinning tops, sharpened our skates, and got bullets out of our 22 rifles. Characteristic of him was the cross current of his speech and action.

Right in the middle of an important task we'd bring him a busted skate, broken bat or pointless top. "What you got now, honey. Ain't never seen such boys since I've been born in my life time in the world. I ain't got time to fool with you."

But all the time he was looking the skate or the bat or top over and off he'd go with that peculiar jerking of his right leg. In no time our troubles were ended.

That he could drive a yoke of oxen set him just a little below the gods. That he hauled freight from the depot also added to his importance, and that occasionally he permitted us to ride atop the mysterious boxes and bales knighted him above Sir Galahad.

No project was undertaken without him having a hand in it whether as adviser, consultant or participant.

Not even a barn was built without his ceremonial attendance. And certainly nothing was destroyed without his active protest. Until late years never a fire occurred but what he was the dominating figure, his voice the prompting behind every effort. As a chronicler of events what Stenter was to Troy, so Doctor to Denmark.

Not only an integral part of the town, he was a part of our lives. In the ten fashioning and growing days to have lost him would have been calamity. He was a privileged character, and his voice rose in heated argument, blasting denunciation or shrilling proclamation was as natural to us as the raising of the sun.

We borrowed most everything we needed from him but his philosophy and, as he said, our religion. Anything he had was ours for the asking. Need a saw, hammer, and axe, go to Doctor Robinson. "Want to get your mule and wagon to haul a load of sand, Doctor." "Alright, honey, but you get them back in time for me to go to the depot."

His philosophy fitted him to his sphere in life: What he didn't have he didn't want. His creed was even more simple "I gosh, honey, it ain't none of my business but" Lending a healing hand and giving a bit of advance even if it wasn't "none of his business." And maybe like the Ancient Mariner he'd corner you and pound it into your stubborn head.

In later years Doc owned a mule named Jenny who understood Doctor's moods better than he did himself. Meet them in the road and you could tell Doctor's temper by the attitude of Jenny. If he was in a good humor she would loaf along apparently listening to the soliloquy Doctor would in all probability be delivering. But if Doctor was out of sorts Jenny would be heading up the road tending strictly to business. "Go long there, mule. You're the dandiest fool mule I ever saw since I've been born in my life time in the world."

A quaint character of a generation when men lived not according to a pattern but individuality, so as to leave upon that generation a distinct characteristic imprint. Having written his brief page Doctor now ¯

"After Life's fitful fever, sleeps well."

Along Rural By-Paths (Dreams)

By FONVILLE NEVILLE

Dreams are peculiar manifestations of something

within us of which we know little, Freud tries to dispel the mystery by saying they are the workings of our subconscious mind. Experiences undergone; happenings, thoughts stored in that vast reservoir of the mind coming to light when we are asleep under the power of that other self.

The ancient explained dreams upon which they placed much prophetic power as the recollection of the soul‾ events which transpired when the soul inhabited another body. If one dreamed that he were a king, the soul he had was at one time in the dim past the soul of a king. Their conception of immortality was that they should never perished but passed from the dead to the living, bringing with it all past experiences which it portrayed in dreams, the subconscious mind perhaps the director.

Freud's theory does not lack ample proof. Some years ago the late W. T. Duncan dreamed the combination of a safe which he had forgotten. Twenty years perhaps had passed before he had need of the safe he had used in earlier days. Rack his brain as he did he could not recall the combination. Then one night he dreamed it.

As the theory of the ancients...

It was almost dusk, June 5th, 1861, and Captain Jim and the Danes were to march at dawn. Molly Womack stood at the gate peering anxiously down the road.

"He said he'd come at dusk," she whispered. "Surely he will."

The evening star peeped out and the road grew dim before it held a horseman coming swiftly.

It was Captain Jim and he flung himself from the horse to catch Molly to him. He made a handsome figure in his new uniform of grey, sash of gold, gleaming sword.

"I thought you had forgotten," whispered Molly.

"Forget you!" he whispered in return. "Life and you are synonymous." He drew her closer. "Sweetheart," he murmured, "there's something I want you to do tonight."

"What."

"Marry me!"

She drew back.

"Please, dear," he urged. "I'm marching away tomorrow and may never come back."

There were two soldier witnesses, and the chaplain. She stood at dawn at a window and watched the Danes

The Ambrose Duncan store in Denmark in 1915. The building was owned by Mr. J. B. Burton. The yearly rent was $90. William Duncan is second person with straw hat on, he was about 17 at the time. The Cyclone of 1909 had destroyed much of the town, at one time there were over 20 stores in Denmark. The Baptist and Methodist Churches were both destroyed but both had rebuilt. Big Black Creek Baptist had used the Denmark Presbyterian Church for several years until the Baptist Church could be rebuilt. The Baptist Church was on the "Big Hill" at the corner of Estonallie Road and Denmark Huntersville Road. The Methodist was down the little road just across from the Baptist. The Methodist Cemetery is still at this site. It is owned by Big Black Creek Historical Association. The Big Black Creek Baptist Cemetery is behind the Stevie Carter house and is also owned by Big Black Creek Historical. www.bigblackcreekhistorical.com Face book: Big Black Creek.

march away, Captain Jim at their head.

He never came back. He never saw the boy baby who looked so much like him. Both soldier witnesses were killed, as was the chaplain. The marriage certificate hidden somewhere by Captain Jim. No one knew where but him and he was dead.

Molly carried the boy to the stern old man on the Hill who had sworn to disinherit Captain Jim if he married her. The scion of the house of Meriweather should not mate with humble clay.

Harsh and cold the old man looked at her. "You say Jim married you the night before he marched. Where's your proof, witnesses, minister?"

She shook her head. He nodded coldly. "Any more fairy tales," he sneered.

She held up the baby–living image of Captain Jim. The old man bent to it–turned pale and started back. Recovering said– "There's no proof that he married you. The child might be his but it had no claim. Go!"

She went back and stood within the gate before which Captain Jim had dismounted to ask her to be his bride. "He thinks–he thinks," she whispered to the same star. Then she lifted her baby up. "There is a God in Heaven. Jim! Jim! You must make it all right."

She dreamed of Captain Jim that night. Sash of golf and gleaming sword, he stood beside her. He tried to tell her something but the stern old man on the Hill came to stand between them.

Some believe Captain Jim married her. Others didn't. But it made no difference. She knew and down the long years she carried the memory as a sentinel against all misfortune. She dreaded, yet welcomed, the day when she have to tell the boy the truth. She knew he would hold what slanderous tongues could fling.

He was eight when she told him.

"I'm Captain Jim's son," he said.

"Yes, dear, truly his son. You're his living image." The lad drew himself up strong and straight.

"And the old man up yonder on the Hill says I'm not."

"He says–he says." Her courage came back. "He says you might be his son, but that Captain Jim never married me."

The next day he slipped away from his mother and went up on the Hill. Hiram Meriweather was sitting in the porch dreaming old dreams and his hawk-like features twisted when there came into his vision a miniature of Captain Jim. His weathered hands trembled on the head of his cane so that he could not stand.

"What are you doing up here?" he croaked.

"I came to see my grandfather."

"You–you–" sputtered the old man.

"I'm Captain Jim's son."

The other laughed mirthlessly.

"You're a damned wood's colt."

The lad looked at him. He had an idea what he meant. "Mother says I'll get my rights because there's a God in Heaven."

"But he don't practice in the courts down here," growled Hiram Meriweather. "Get home you young scamp and don't come back here again."

The lad stood straight, his blue eyes burning. "Mother don't know I'm here. She said she'd bring me to see you when you were dead."

The old man started violently, "Dead! Dead!" Then he laughed harshly. "Tell your mother she may bring you to look on my dead face but she'll never bring to you the name of Meriweather."

A year later his mother brought him back to Hiram Meriweather's funeral–Captain Jim's blue eyes and tawny hair. In blood but lacked the name. He looked curiously at the withered, bitter face. To his mother he said, "I'm the only Meriweather left now."

She looked at him and saw only truth in his eyes. Through them she seemed to hear Captain Jim calling. "He'll make it right," she whispered. She felt the message in those eyes but could not read it.

That night his mother found him sitting up in bed staring about, bewildered. "I thought," he muttered, "that I was in another room–a great big room with lots of books all around the wall. Somebody–he stopped, puzzled, "somebody told me I had put something in a book there a long time ago and must go back and get it."

"You were dreaming, son," said Molly. "Go back to sleep."

What there was to hope for in attending the reading of the last will of Hiram Meriweather was her son, and armed with this knowledge she would defy all scorn and shame to make one last fight for him.

Dully she listened to the reading; the naming of bequests to this and that relative. Finally it came to an end. The lawyer cleared his throat glanced at Molly. "Just a few days before Mr. Meriweather's death he added a codicil to the will to the effect that Captain Jim had a son by marriage and that son should become heir to the entire estate."

So old Hiram Meriwaether had a sense of justice after all!

Molly felt the lawyer's eyes on her. "Your son," he said, "you claim to be the grandson of Hiram Meriweather?"

"He is the grandson of Hiram Meriweather."

"Why did not Mr. Meriweather recognize him as such?"

"Because I could not furnish him proof of our wedding."

"Have you any proof to present now?"

The silence was awkward. Some turned scornful

eyes upon her, others looked away in empathy. "I have only my boy and my word."

"Mother!"

The lad had slipped from his mother's side, staring with wide eyes about the library which he had seen for the first time. "Mother," he cried. "This is the room I dreamed I was in the other night."

Slowly like one in a dream he crossed the room to an old book case. Mechanically he opened the glass door and stood for a moment, studying the books. He pulled one out ̄Tan Houser.

It fell open at a place and a paper fluttered to the floor. The lawyer picked it up – glanced quickly at it and handed it to Molly. "Your marriage certificate," he said. "It is all the proof you need."

Wandering through the old cemetery the other day I came upon the grave of Molly Meriweather. The stone bore her name, date of birth and death and a three word superscripting. Simple, yet eloquent enough for a thousand sermons. A tribute to a woman's constancy. "I kept faith," it says.

* * *

THE HARDEE'S OF DENMARK, TENNESSEE

All through its history the Hardee's have played a major role in its history. Probably the first to migrate to West Tennessee and Denmark was Lemuel. Lemuel was born 18 October 1838 in Johnston County, North Carolina to Major John Hardee and Elizabeth Mewborn. Lemuel married Aphia Adeline Utley in North Carolina before the birth of their first child William Archie Hardee on 11 August 1859. Lemuel and Aphia migrated to West Tennessee and settled in Denmark. It is not known why they made Madison County their home. Lemuel purchased 79 acres of land on 13 Mar. 1863 from W. L. Utley in the amount of fourteen hundred dollars where he and Aphia made their home on Estonallie Road.

The country's Civil War was in full swing and growing closer to home. Aphia was eigh months pregnant with their third child, Lucy, when Lemuel enlisted in the Confederacy on 8 Jul 1863 in Denmark during a raid behind Federal lines.

Lemuel served in the 14th Tennessee Cavalry lead by J. J. Neely. He was still with the unit at the War's end and was paroled in Brownsville, Tennessee, on 31 May

1865 as a Prisoner of War.

Aphia died 11 Sept. 1872 after giving birth to their last daughter, all are buried in the Denmark Presbyterian Cemetery. After Aphia's death Lemuel Adeline F. Winston on 17th Feb. 1873. *Jackie Utley*

Mr. Robert and Mrs. Altha Ruth Hardee

Mr. Robert Hardee was born in Denmark, Sept. 17, 1914, he graduated from Huntersville High School. Served in the 451st Army Engineers from 1942 to 1945 in Africa and Italy, he married Mrs. Alta Ruth Montgomery, he meet Alta Ruth on a blind date, they had three children, Sylvia Hardee Dimarco, Rayna Hardee Bomar and David Hardee. He took over his fathers grocery store. His father David McNeil Hardee who had run the store for 40 years. He was by friends as uniquely humble and dignified. He was elected to the Madison County Court in 1942 where he served for 50 years. Mr. Robert died in 1955.

Rayna Hardee Bomar and Hugh Bomar Wedding
Denmark Presbyterian Church
November 27, 1982
Pictured: Mr. And Mrs David Bomar
Hugh Bomar/Rayna Hardee Bomar
Mr. And Mrs. Robert Hardee

Denmark Moonshiners

As told by Johney Peters

Mr. Peters says it is a true story that when Mr. Dave Hardee owned the grocery store in Denmark during the depression he kept a sugar barrel from which he sold sugar by the pound, or otherwise according to customers' needs. Local moonshiners visited the store and determined the exact location of the sugar barrel, then returned at night to crawl underneath the store and drill a hole through the floor and into the bottom of the sugar barrel. When Mr. Hardee opened the barrel to obtain sugar for a customer, he was surprised to find that there was no sugar left in the barrel. The moonshiners had drained it dry.

Mrs. Alta Ruth Hardee

Mrs. Alta Ruth was born Sept. 22, 1927. She had married Mr. Robert June 22, 1950. She graduated from the Jackson High School in 1945, and attended Lambuth College, she became a teacher, but in 1971 she became the postmaster in Denmark and held that position until her death. She was a charter member of the Denmark

Historical Society. If it had not been for her and Mrs. Louise Stevens we would not have the Denmark Presbyterian Church, these two ladies were determined that this Church would survive, even going before the Presbyterian Synod to plead the case.

* * *

From: Mr. Fonville Neville

To: Mrs Louise Stevens on her sixteenth birthday

I have no song to sing you,
Old age had no song to sing
To skies so dull and gray;
But ere you grow older,
One lesson I would give you
For every day.

Be good sweet maid,
Let those who will, be cleaver.
Do noble deeds, not dream them
all day long.
And make of life, death,
And the vast forever,
One grand sweet song.
From Mr. Fonville Neville
To Louise

* * *

"The Town of Yesterday"

The moonbeams fall very gently o'er the Old Town of the Past

And I seem to hear them whisper, "Time is fleeing, fleeing fast."

And the sunlight lingers softly o'er some well-beloved spot

Like a benediction which murmurs "Not forgot."

Night is drawing, drawing close on the Old Town of the Past

And the days are growing short and the end I near at last

But when night does come and the Old Town fades away,

There will be for'r a memory of the Old Town of Yesterday.

Fonville Neville Papers, Union University

* * *

A Britton Lane Incident

By FONVILLE NEVILLE

Probably the briefest enlistment in the Federal army took place in the fight at Britton's Lane.

One mile north over the Big Hill is the Reid place, one of the oldest houses in the country and built on the order of The Briers, the onetime home of Jeff Davis.

Jim Reid lives there. His grandfather, Jim Reid built it, slightly remembered by the writer. A small man, very mercurial tempered. Lost an arm in the Mexican War.

It has at one time a large oak shaded lawn where the Yankees bivouacked frequently. But it was known they avoided Uncle Jimmy, or Uncle Jeems, like a hornet's nest.

Colonel William Faulkner, grandfather of the novelist, made headquarters there for a short time at the war's beginning. The Federals moving in swiftly almost captured him. He escaped through a back window clad only in his underwear and hat.

One of the Reid boys, there were five, started one day to Denmark, riding his pony and a muchly prized saddle. Ascending the Big Hill he ran into a small troop of Federal cavalry who immediately surrounded him demanding his pony and saddle.

Young Reid knew the country intimately. A brush screen side raid was at hand. No way minded to give up the saddle he spurred into the side road.

The race led past the old Wilson house. A young girl, Callie Wilson, attracted by the shooting, hoof beats, shots the Yankees fired over the head of the fleeing youth, witnessed it from a window until a bullet imbedded itself in the wall, another in the chimney.

Pressed closely young Reid again detoured. Coming to what we always called the Sand Branch he abandoned his pony, took the prized saddle and hid in a clump of bushes. The Yankee collected the pony and didn't bother to search for him.

Uncle Sam, we called him, one time slave of Master Jeems, as he called Uncle Jimmy, bearing the ancestral name, lived in our time a short distance down the depot road in the discarded Presbyterian Manse.

Too old for labor when we knew him, Uncle Sam loved nothing better than to set on the long steps across the front of Scrap Burton's store and talk of the old days, chief of which was the time he joined the Federal army.

He was sixteen years old at the time of the Britton's Lane fight. The day before, the detachment of cavalry which had taken part in the fight, had passed along the road by the Reid place.

Often with a boy's curiosity he had watched the Federals pass, afraid of them but admiring their uniform, envying what seemed to him their care free existence. Odors from their mess as they had bivouacked on the front lawn had tantalized his nostrils and made hungry his stomach.

Pulling fodder that hot August day he had gone to the rail fence to watch them ride by. One of the troopers seeing in him excellent material for a camp roustabout rode up to the fence. He was to the best of Uncle Sam's recollection a corporal.

"Come on, nigger, and go with us. Your folks are going to be whipped pretty soon and you'll land in jail if you're not shot. We'll make a soldier out of you and give you plenty to eat."

"Marse Jeems would whip the life outer me," said Sam.

"Ain't no whipping going to be done now. No fodder to pull. All you'll have to do is curry horses, water them, sleep and eat." He tossed the young Negro a cap.

Uncle Sam said he wouldn't have gone with the Yankees if it hadn't been for that cap. Gold braided, it fit his curly head well. No fodder to pull, only horses to feed, water and curry.

"We'll give you a uniform," said the trooper.

That did it! Sam scrambled over the fence, climbed up behind the soldier. However, not without misgivings and many a backward look to see if Marse Jeems wasn't following.

Uncle Sam remembered they camped that night in the Presbyterian church yard, a commodious place sheltered by a number of mulberry trees . .He also recollected they were searching for a member of Forrest's cavalry, home on furlough, which they had almost caught earlier in the day.

Sam had carried a countless number of buckets of water for the troopers and horses from the Henry Tavern cistern not knowing the Forrest trooper was watching him from an upstairs window of the church. Sam was given a uniform of sorts. That it fitted only in places bothered him not at all. He was as proud as Lucifer.

The troop was joined the next morning by what seemed to Sam to be the whole United States army and two cannons and they all put out for Medon where there had been a fight the day before.

Folks were getting ready to go to church when they went through Denmark. It was hot and dusty. By the middle of the morning they came to a narrow lane. There was a corn field and a rail fence on one side, a clump of trees on the other. The road ran down into a slight ravine. Where it came out it vanished from sight around a curve. Above the trees beyond the curve Sam thought he saw a cloud of dust.

A young slave, Bryant Britton, chattel of the Britton Brothers, was pulled from a briar patch. Scared so badly he could hardly talk, he told that a Confederate force was just ahead.

No sooner had the young Negro finished than Sam heard a trooper exclaim, "There's the Johnnies now." He saw grey figures breaking out of the wood on the other side of the corn field. They came through the corn from which the fodder had been pulled.

Uncle Sam couldn't remember how many times the

Confederates tried to take the fence behind which lay the Federal infantry. They'd come slow at first, and half way they'd break into a run and, yelling, charge. The cavalry had dismounted and joined the infantry. Sam was among the horse holders.

The minnies sounded like nothing else on earth. They didn't zip but came with a keening sound that curdled his blood. A horse was hit. Another, and Sam got down on his stomach. But he was confident the "Rebels" wouldn't take the fence. "Us Nunited States soljers couldn't be whupped." Two cannons and all them men! No sir!

The charge through the corn field stopped. Silent heat was oppressive. Sam remembers standing up and looking at the dead soldiers on the other side of the fence. Then down the road around the curve arose a faint yelling, the drumming of hoofs.

The yelling grew louder; the hoof beats became a roar. Sam heard that yell before. Had used it himself in the briar patch and sage field when a rabbit was jumped.

Dust boiled up. The curve in the road was filled with a wave if grey that came swiftly, filling the narrow road from edge to edge. Into the ravine it flowed, then out again, grey men and horses⁻riding down on the two guns which were on the right of the Federal line.

The line of infantry began to turn back upon itself. The muzzles of two cannon were shifted from the corn fields to the road, sighted, sponged out, powder rammed home. Canister⁻

Some of the gunner's faltered⁻blundered. One of the rammers was lost, a gunner dropped a firing pin.

Forty yards away the grey wave was eating up the road, grey clothed demons in a veil of dust. Thirty yards! Twenty. Each grey demon hunched over his saddle horn, yelling, bringing gun to the fore. Reins in his teeth!

Right then and there Sam resigned from the Federal army. Nothing, nobody could whip them Southern gentlemen! In fact, his resignation came a little later than his feet had decreed. He was well on his way home at about twenty miles an hour when it came to his mind.

"Us sho did whup dem Yankees," he told Marse Jeems that afternoon, pulling fodder as he never pulled it before. Marse Jeems looked down on him from his horse, noting his enthusiasm for work which Sam had never previously shown. Yet he glared at Sam. "Us? The last time I saw you. you was riding off with the Yankees."

"Yassah. I wuz jes' leading' 'em to wher Genl Forrest could get a good whack at dem." Uncle Sam had a low chuckling laugh. "Uv course Marse Jeems knowed I wuz lying, and he knowed my fling wid dem Yankees wuz worth mo' den a dozen whuppin's. he jes' grinned and rode on."

* * *

West Tennessee Whig Friday, May 17, 1861
"Mustered in"
"The Danes" Captain John Ingram, First Lieut.

Frances W. Campbell, Second Lieut. Vacant, Third Lieut James Walker.

* * *

We believe there are 21 Civil War soldiers buried at Britton Lane, and there are 28 buried at Hayes Chapel Cemetery in a trench. There are at least 415 veterans from all wars buried in the Big Black Creek Community, a ten mile radius around Denmark. We have located over 47 cemeteries in the community. Some of the cemeteries with large number of veterans are, Maple Springs Baptist 101, St. John Baptist, 30, Ararat Baptist, 30, Woodland Baptist, 24, Denmark Presbyterian, 22, Blair Chapel CME, 20, just to name a few. Cemetery reading, 2014.

The Maple Springs Baptist Church

Mr. Fuller gave Preacher Obediah Dodson five acres of land and $500 to build this church. Mr. Fuller and his slaves had been attending the Big Black Creek Baptist Church and he wanted a church closer to his plantation. The only stipulation was it had to have a slave balcony. Mr. Fuller had been a Quaker before moving to Tennessee. The building was built in about 1823.

A Negro man came through Denmark carrying a payroll during the Civil War; he got sick and died. He was buried in the N.E. corner of Presbyterian Cemetery.

Florence Hardee

* * *

Sun Forum

I hate change of any sort with all the intensity of the proverbial British, not that it affects in any material way my private life, but in some subtle ways affects the facets of the world that I live in.

There are changes that affect my spiritual world; more specifically, there are changes that change the very atmosphere of the things one had lived with so long.

This is the reason that I regret to hear of David Murray's impending retirement from the office of district attorney.

For as long as I can remember, and my memory runs back to many cycles of Jackson and Madison County history, Baltimore Street has proclaimed the domain of Murrays, and the street will not be the same without the

THE JOHN B. INGRAM BIVOUAC - UNITED CONFEDERATE VETERANS

The John Ingram Bivouac held their meetings in the new Carnegie Library after it was opened in 1903. One of the highlights of the year was to attend a big reunion. This picture was taken at the north door of the Madison County Courthouse on July 18, 1890, just before the men took the train for a big reunion at Atlanta, Georgia. Pictured here from left to right (also by numbers) are: 1-Capt. James Dinkins, 2-1st Lt. L. E. Talbot, 3-2nd Lt. William Holland, 4-Sgt. W. L. Utley, *5-Cpl. C. C. Bond, 6-Pvt. Joe Tidwell, 7-J. G. Williamson, 8-John Robinson, 9-W. W. Gates, 10-Robert Bryant, 11-T. M. Hartmus, 12-D. Cole, 13-John Stovall, 14-W. A. Maulden, 15-W. F. Henry, 16-Frank Quin Yancey, 18-Joe M. Mulherron, 19-William Griffin, 20-D. M. McCutchen, 21-Charles Owen, 22-T. J. Barnes, 23-W. F. Alexander, 24-Joe Griffin, 25-Frank Talley, 26-Raz Mercer, 27-W. A. Mercer, 28-Harold Bond, ten year old child of the company.*

JOHN B. INGRAM, BIVOUAC #5, CAMP #219
JACKSON, TN. 38301

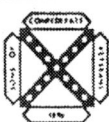

Sons of Confederate Veterans

sign of Murray inhabiting the door of an office ⎯ unpretentious as that door seems before it gathered both the common people and the notables of West Tennessee and all found a mutual welcome.

It has been a door plain enough in its design but very significant of the personality that has given it the dignity and warm friendship that have existed so long behind it, not to mention the talent that has also added more luster to the name Murray.

Fonville Neville

Denmark

* * *

Denmark Church Service Reminds of Other Days

By FONVILLE NEVILLE

Denmark's historic Presbyterian Church had a gathering Sunday reminiscent if its youth, when it was the religious and cultural center of the community.

The aged pews held a congregation like the old days to hear Mrs. Roland Harris and Andrew Chapel Methodist

Church's Junior Choir. Mrs. Eloise Meriwether was at the piano.

Born in a brush arbor on Cub Creek in 1827, the Denmark church grew from three charter members. Its present two-story building was erected at Denmark in 1854.

The Rev. James Gillespie served it before the war for 25 year, preaching each Sunday and drawing what in those days was a munificent salary, $1,200.

One hundreds sixty members contributed to his support and most of them occupied their pews every Sabbath. Every family had a private pew and a small gate shut it off from strangers. The mulberry shaded churchyard glistened with shining carriages, tassel-topped barouches and coaches, the satiny skins of horses, and Negro drivers.

Its five elders, fixed in the courage and admonition of the Holy Scriptures were stern in their discipline as an old session's book disclosed. Immorality was not excused in any manner and such minor offenses as tippling ¯ that is, selling liquor, drinking, gambling, and dicing, and dancing were severely dealt with, the culprits given a chance to repent and reform or else were turned out of the church.

In some cases where the recalcitrant was a bit stubborn, his or her case was carried from session to session in some hope of reformation.

In its walls May 5, 1862, Dr. Will Caldwell preached a farewell sermon to the Denmark Danes, and a flag made by the ladies of the church was presented by Miss Mary Gray. Under its fold and with the blessing of the venerable pastor, the Danes marched to Jackson, thence to Camp Beauregard and from there to the bloody field of Shiloh.

In 1862 two if Forest's men, home on leave, attended church services. They were trapped by a squad of Federal troopers. They hid in the pew in which they were sitting, concealed beneath the hoopskirts of their sweethearts.

Following the service, the crowd "repaired" (as they said in the 1850's) to the home of Mrs. Freeman Hardee where cookies, cakes, soft drinks, and coffee were served.

The Andrews Chapel Methodist Church started out as Andrews Chapel Methodist Episcopal South. It was founded in about 1820 by Dr. Harvey Crittenden and Mr. John Merriwether. It is almost as old as the

Denmark Presbyterian. There are two cemeteries connected with the Church, the one beside the Church and one just off the Denmark/Huntersville Road where the Merriwethers and Crittendens are buried. There is a marker of a slave there. The slaves were members of the Church. The Hayes Chapel Methodist Episcopal Church was organized about this same time. It's site is on Hwy. 138. The cemetery is there. Mr. Miles Hayes gave this land for the Church and cemetery, his only request was that he be given a burial spot. There are 38 Confederate Troop buried in a mass grave here. This Church merged with Mercer Methodist when that Church was organized. Mr. Franklin McGlathery helped organize this congregation. He is one of the founders of Mercer. The town was supposed to be named McGlathery, but no one could spell or pronounce it. He had married Mattie Mercer, so they chose Mercer. Franklin and Mattie built a home in Mercer in 1888 and he became the Train Station Master. Mattie died in 1900 and is buried in the Maple Springs Cemetery.

* * *

Requiescat, Mrs. So and So
By Fonville Neville

She is grown now, Mrs. So-and-So' that land of make believe
This lured her baby feet into paths of fairy weave
No longer colors life; she's entering the door
That leads away from childhood; its dreams will come no
more.

Her baby feet are strong, they're stealing away from me
From the harbor of my arms for an adventurer to be.
Her golden hair a-blowing, a new light in her eyes;
Fanned by the winds of purpose, lured by distant skies.

There is now no lisping voice, no twisted words to flower
In that garden in my heart where she roamed-happy bower.
Its name was Hope, 'tis now named Memory; 'tis marked
every place
By a blue-eyes toddling babe with a lady's air and grace.

She cuddles now no longer in the arms that sought to hold
To keep her as my baby with her sweetness rare as gold.
They ache now with emptiness; my eyes search to and fro
For a stately little lady who was named Mrs. So-and-So.

When the even-shadows touch my window I wander
everywhere
To avoid the haunting picture of a little rocking chair
In which she sat so solemnly when she played at make-
believe
And climbed with the feet of imagery a stair of fairy weave.

In the quaintest of gowns and bonnets with a manner
befittingly rare-
A shell-like ear peeping playing from a wealth of golden
hair-
The purple of the autumn hills, the blue of April skies,
Blended with silver water to show the beauty of her eyes.

A picture framed by Time to be hallowed and enshrined
On the pinnacle of Memory when her youth is left behind.
A vision that will lighten every turning of a page
When life shall write so harshly on the tablet of old age.

A picture! Can it fill these arms that reach in vain
For a little baby girl who will never come again?
Memory may dull, but it cannot fill, I know,
The place that aches with emptiness for Mrs. So-and-So.

The winds will whisper of her, every sound it makes will
frame
Through roses or barren branches the lullaby of her name;
The people nights will etch, shadows cannot erase-
Through the veil of maturity I shall see her baby face.

In that land of make-believe, in that garden where she
dwelled,
I will enter there alone and by Memory I shall be held,
To weave with broken threads, with lifeless paint draw
slow
A stately little lady who was named Mrs. So-and-So.

Concerning Ghosts - 1955

(A Halloween story by Fonville Neville of Denmark, Tenn.)

A long time ago in Denmark there was a fellow who didn't believe in ghosts.

Which was a bit unusual because then the most intelligent of folks had a sneaking suspicion, if not a certainty, that such things existed, even though they wouldn't admit it.

No cars, no radio, picture shows or TV's, folks had to find or make their own entertainment; it was an era of storytelling, the chief of which was a well told ghost tale. Roads mostly through heavy forests, cane and bush lined bottoms, in uninhibited sections, wild life and who knows what else abounded, and it is not to be seriously questioned but what the night traveler saw and heard much to incline him to such beliefs.

This man was quite an important citizen, a justice of the peace to be exact, and it was his custom to scoff at such childish ideas. There were times when he went so far as to say they were the product of ignorant minds.

The headless woman which floated silently through the night above the head of the lone traveler on what was known locally as the Locust Lane; the two story house out on the Mount Taber road filled according to ear witnesses with rattling chains, horrible growns and shrieks, ghostly things which flew bat-like moving like cats from the windows, the light which appeared at certain intervals on the Big Hill where a man, murdered for his buried gold, comes back to guard it against all seekers; and the lass who walks without feet carrying a jack o' lantern in her hand, along the Britton Lane road when the night wind snarls through the old trees, searching for the lover she betrayed to death.

Just tall tales, he'd say, born of too much association with darkies, children's stuff we hadn't outgrown. He could have been right, especially the children's stuff we hadn't outgrown.

Doubtless we didn't believe in them as much as we cherished them, since from our infancy we had heard them told. They had grown into legends with the magic of the stars we saw but didn't understand.

We had no evidence that they were not true - or

were true. What was more important we wanted such things as ghosts and "haunts" to exist. Who can say of how much disbelief in them, a cold appraisal of them, would have robbed life of? Steeped in their verity night will have lost its mystery and its sights and sounds carried on its breath wouldn't have aroused a single throb of fear, and though we pictured each waving bush, any untoward shadow, a faint echo, the rustling of a leaf, with fear, that fear was not of physical violence but of the unknown which carried a thrill all of its own.

None of us will ever forget the memory of a huge fireplace, glowing with embers, the light of which played fitfully over black faces and white, sweet 'taters roasting in the ashes, the wind murmuring outside, rain whispering against the shutters, the soft voice of the story teller, suiting his worlds to the turn of the story, his seemed black face picturing its emotions. We heard the groans, the shrieks, the rattle of chains, saw ghostly shadows, headless or with hideous faces, all with a thrill of fear which held us enthralled.

No background of any age or time ever equaled this! It is a mystery that it wove an indelibly bright thread in the warp and woof or our lives?

No session was ever complete without a talk about

The Britton Lane School cross the road from
Britton Lane Battle Field.

the fabulous and mythical hounds, more famous in Negro lore than the hound of the Baskerville's on detective fiction.

They roamed the night unseen but sometimes from a distant hill their baying could be heard deep, mournful– and fear begetting. That is, of course, if one had the ears to hear.

The old Negro would pause sometimes put a hand to his ear. "Seems lak ah hyerd 'em den." What a delightful thrill of fear shook us from hounds, Sollymo and Dollymo.

It was a long time afterwards before we came to the knowledge that these mythical hounds were symbols in a simple and inimitable portrayal of that powerful guide post of human conduct–conscience.

Whatever the chief character had done there always was the same ending–the survival of right over wrong.

"De mean fellow id all he meanness cooped up in 'im 'ould git in he cabin an' be'lieve he wuz hid an' de durt he'd done 'ould never out. He's shut de doh an' tek his case. Den torectly way of yonder he'd hyar, 'I-o-u-g-h. i-o-u-g-h. i-o-u-g—uh.'"

"Maybe hit wuz er possum dawg he'd say tuh hisself; maybe a fox houn'. He'd sot right still en listen."

"He'd hyar hit ergin, 'I-o-u-g-h, i-ou-u-g-h, i-o-u-g—uh.'"

"Ain't no yuther dawgs howled lak dem houn's; dey bark seemed tuh be in de air, in de groun—everywhar. En he'd sot en lissen mo. Ofen dem houn's wuz runnin' faster dan de win' he'd know he wuz done!"

Almost as frightened as the picture miscreant we sat and listened and shook to our shoes, picturing those enormous ghostly dogs racing with the speed of the wind through the night.

"De fello' barred de dog an' de shutters; he got down he gun."

"Fohe he knowed what wuz gwyin on dere wuz two pairs uv eyes, big ed saucers, lookin' right through the cabin wall at 'im."

"He banged at dem; dey looked at him from de yuther side. He banged ergin but dey kept starin' at him, an' he knowed right den an' dar dere wuz nuthin' he could do tuh drive dem erway but tuh git right outer dere an' undone what he had done."

On long winter nights sometimes we pause and think we can hear Dollymo and Sollymo baying from the distant hill.

Science and sophistication have banished these dear illusions, but the memory of them remain. Never the moon hangs just above the tree tops on a mist drenched night but what we believe there are elves dancing in its beams, and no lonely, silent, empty house but had its prowling shadows of the past, ghostly shadows of the past which would not see but feel.

Hallowe'en eve then was more observed than now; every holiday was more truthfully observed then than now. There was no artifice, no substitution. Fun was the guiding spirit and masquerade its chief ingredient to that end.

Costumes were not bought. Homemade, they had to be deviled and constructed according to the genius of the wearer, and of course they were varied, sometimes very queer, and very simple.

On this particular Hallowe'en eve when the Squire was baptized onto the elect of ghost believers, his son arrayed himself perforce in the only costume he could contrive-a bed sheet and the Squire's derby.

He was treading on thin ice. That derby was the Squire's proudest attire. But he thought the extingencies of the occasion was worth the risk.

One of his buddies was handy with chalk and he sketched on top of the derby the likeness of a human skull–perfect portrait of "poor Yorick."

To the derby was tied a string to go beneath the chin. Wrapped in the sheet, the derby dropped down over his face, he created quite a startling character for Hallowe'en.

The party over the young man on his way home, a bit elated over the success his outfit had drawn wondered how he might further enhance his honors and there came to him knowledge of a certain rendezvous, a gully back of Scrap Burton's store, the dry clay floor of which was an excellent table for crap shooting.

There was gathered around in a circle the dusky devotees of the game beneath a lantern hung from a swinging limb. One was calling for his point to come home so he could buy the baby a pair of shoes when the young fellow stepped into the edge of the light, spread out the sheet, dropped the death's head derby over his face and shrieked!

It took a whole day for the dust to settle. Marks can yet be seen where the undergrowth was uprooted and bark knocked off the trees. Another ghost tale was born. Crap shooting went to a lower ebb than ever induced by big meetings.

At home the young fellow, tired and yearning for bed, thoughtlessly hung the caricatured derby by its string on the hat rack on the back porch. Beneath the derby he hung the sheet and to bed he went.

That he had without permission slipped out the derby was due to a meeting that night of the Masonic lodge of which the Squire was a member. It came to an end, the country members making the night clamorous with their departure in buggies and on saddle. Not an unusual departure by any means, for there was never a lodge meeting without it success being assured by certain spirits which were not certainly of the ghostly kind, so there was much shouting, racing and dust raising. The Squire lived only a short distance from hall which was over the Presbyterian Church, took such part in the home going as he could, his portly form and falsetto bass not allowing much latitude. After the manner of men since time immemorial coming home from a late lodge meeting, he slipped around to the back.

He eased around the corner, stepped quickly past the back window by which sat a lamp turned low, and was about to mount the steps when a slight scrubbing noise attracted his attention. He looked up just as a gust of wind lifted the derby to face him.

It was dropped as quickly by the wind. The Squire saw it and he didn't see it. He shook his head to clear his vision - looked again, and not seeing anything but a vague shadow where the sheet hung assayed the steps again.

A half-moon came out from behind a cloud; the prankish wind lifted the derby, and this time widened the sheet with a ghostly rustling. And at the same instant a courting tom cat under the porch called his mate with an earthly screech.

The steps were suddenly, very suddenly, vacated, and there was a strange fluttering in the night.

After so long a time when the Squire didn't show up, the Mrs. routed the youngster out of bed, put a lantern in his hand, and started him in a search for his dad.

He made the rounds of the neighborhood, visited barns, pig pens and hen houses but no dad. He enlarged the circle. One of the most distant neighbors had heard a queer sound out back. They looked up a tree observed they'ed seen some mighty big owls but none like this, and there was the Squire twenty feet up a hickory tree.

They had to plant a ladder to get him down; he couldn't say how he got up there. Through curiosity he was tracked the next morning. Judging from the debris along the route he took it was evident that the tree had gotten in his way; there was no time to go around so he went up.

He was escorted by his son home. When they approached the back he became peculiarly alert. He mounted the steps looking for something but all he saw – the Mrs. in the interest of her son's welfare had removed the derby and sheet –what the Squire saw was the hat swinging idly and unoccupied by the wind.

"I'll be damned!" he muttered.

He apologized to the boy and hastily entered the house.

Ever after when ghosts were the topic the Squire was as mum as a pot. And incidentally after lodge meeting he came home as sober as a judge and always entered the front.

* * *

Why Old Denmark Hill Was Not Leveled In Long Ago – August 30, 1953

By FONVILLE NEVILLE

If a certain citizen of long ago Denmark were living today, he would have no trouble sitting on his front porch and looking as he wished into the very heart of the village. Our new black top road of which we are very proud and for which we are duly grateful now stretched like a shining black ribbon from the forks of the road in which his house stood through the village with but slight undulations in its surface, offering no obstruction to one's eye. But as it seems in this life, an unanswerable fact, we must buy what we get in one way or another. No hill would obstruct his eye but now there are but small things to be seen in the village.

There once stood between his house and the village a vision obstructing hill. It was little thought of when his years were light and he could make the daily journey, a quarter of a mile, to the village to sit on the front porch of Scrap Burton's store and add to his book of human wisdom further vagaries of the human race. But when the journey became of more trouble than it granted him pleasure, he had to watch the world from the veranda of his colonial home, and although much of it passed him on both aides down the Estaunaula Ferry Road and the middle Brownsville road, it was like sparks from the main fire which centered in the village. He wanted to view the roots of things. Then one day he came suddenly to the conclusion that if the hill was removed he could see right into the town itself – see the beginning of the county, he set about having the hill removed.

But he was not to do this unopposed.

Sometime before a prosperous planter had moved to the village, buying a place which sat back from the road on an extension of the hill which was fated for removal, and infinitesimal as the reason might seem to some minds, one reason for the purchasing of this place was this same hill. Retiring from active farm life, with an increase of girth which impeded walking any distance, tired of the loneliness of plantation life, he would be able to sit on his front veranda and watch the world pass over the hill. Because of this hill nothing passed that he did not see, the equipage of the wealthy, the ox teams of the poor, the freight wagons from the ferry, the white and black, the flotsam and jetsam of a main traveled road. Many a long summer's day he had passed in this enjoyment and what otherwise would have been a dull existence became an enlivened one.

Then he was awakened one morning by confusion at his front gate–a hurrying about of striped clad figures, thuds of picks being driven in the hard ground, the rasp of shovels as they tossed it into the wagons. Throwing on his clothes he made what haste his bulk allowed to the gate.

For a moment he could hardly believe his eyes, seeing the destruction being wrought on his hill! "What's going on here?" he demanded without the preliminaries of a greeting to a man who carried a shot gun in the crook of his arm who jerked his head in the direction of another man in the other side of the road. He came over, knowing his questionnaire slightly by name. he replied pleasantly. It wasn't good for his job to add to the obstreperousness of a man as prominent in politics as he was in girth as was his interrogator. It was clearly apparent what was being done, but he answered, "Good morning, suh. We're cutting down this hill."

"Why, why, you can't do that!" sputtered the large one. "Confound it you can't do that!"

"Those are my orders, suh."

"Can't help your orders, my man. This is my hill, I gads, and you're–and you're…"

"You own this part of the road, suh?" with the question came up lifted eyebrows.

"No, confound it, I don't own the road. I bought this house on the hill so I could sit on my front veranda and watch the folks go by. I don't get around much and if you cut his hill down to a level with the road I'll see nothing but their dust. It is not so steep but that any kind of load can be hauled over. If you want dirt you can get all you want on the back side of my place.

The gang boss shook his head. "It's not just the dirt, suh. I just got orders to cut it down and haul the dirt away."

"Who gave you those confounded orders, I gads?"

"The road commissioner of the district, suh."

"You just stop work right now! Don't move a tool. I'll go see him at once. I gads, I got a little influence in this country, you'll see."

"But, suh…"

"I'll take full responsibility, I gads. Got so a man can't call his soul his own anymore what with a commissioner this and commissioner that robbing folks of their natural heritage. Cutting down a hill no doubt just for the fun of it, I gads. Well, I'll show 'em."

He started back to the house when the citizens who had started the whole idea and who had witnessed the birth of the trouble from his front veranda strolled up in all the nonchalance of an innocent bystander. "Good morning, gentlemen," he said beaming. "Ah, some road work going on. It is good to see that the county has our interest at heart in removing this unsightly hill."

The other man leaned over his gate, his face becoming a bit purple with suppressed rage. "And just when did this hill become unsightly?"

"Well, ah, it has been not only unsightly but an obstruction to profess," murmured the other. He waved a hand. "There's such a thing as serenity in physical things. A vehicle coming from the village rapidly might top the hill and run down a pedestrian, or a running horse– Humph!"

"Fiddle sticks," roared the other.

"All rot! The hill is not that high."

"It might be obstructing someone's view who is as good a citizen as you."

"And whose view might that be?" There was strong

suspicion in the tones.

"Well, there are several of us at this end of town that would like to see what is going on down there. Humph!"

"And this hill is the mote they want removed so they can see better. When I moved here I bought this place of property on this hill so I could see what was going on, not having the time to be gadding about. If this hill is cut down I'd have to use a periscope, I gads, and I gads, it's not going to be moved."

"But, suh—" began the foreman of the chain gang, "My orders."

"You must obey your orders," said the second citizen.

The foreman cast a quick look at the large obstreperous figure leaned over the gate. "Yes, suh. But, suh—"

"You don't want to lose your job."

"Oh, no, suh!" he lifted a hand to signal the beginning of the work of destruction and one of the striped figures struck a pick in the ground.

The obstreperous one pointed a finger at this friend.

"You have a hand in this knavery?"

"I am not one to obstruct the march of progress. "If it is necessary for this hill to be removed I'd be the last one to say nay."

"Get to work boys," shouted the foreman bold now that he had a champion.

"Wait!" cried the bulky one at the gate.

"You've got your duty to do," urged the other. "But, humph I must not get involved in this. It means nothing to me," and suitable action to words he made off not losing sight of the fact that his friend at the gate had suddenly started for the house is such haste which had in it a premonition of a storm.

Before a dozen shovelfuls of dirt had been thrown a voice was crying again from the gate. The obstreperous one stood there with a loaded barreled army musket in his hand, "Hold everything! Just hold everything," he said softly–too softly. "Put your gang in those waggins and get out of town and don't come back, orders or no orders!"

In view of the fact that he, as it was said, had five men under him due to his skillful shooting this small delay in the moving on. He had joined the Rebel army when he was a mere kid from tory ridden section of the state. After the war he had returned and they had tried to bushwhack him and five of them paid for the attack with their lives. So he was a man who was not to be ignored especially when he gives the orders with a loaded barrel gun in his hands.

No more attempts were made to remove the hill again, it was lost after the death of both before it was only partly cut down. What this last wood building program it had remembered cute test money to die somewhat foolish idea.

* * *

ESTONALLIE/ESTAUNEULA

There are many spellings of Estonallie, the word itself means, "Here We Cross,:" in the Chickasaw language. Some of the earliest writing of Estonallie appear in some of the first newspapers of Tennessee. It was a Chickasaw trading place with the French. They would come up the Mississippi from New Orleans, then up the Hatchie to Estonallie to trade furs. That may have been as early as 1492. When the land grants started in

1818 some of our settlers came up the Hatchie River (Hatchie is also a Chickasaw word meaning, "river,") to get to their land grants. Mr. John Rice, the Pirtle Family, and probably the Harbert family, they would come down the Ohio to the Mississippi, then the Hatchie. As Denmark was growing so was Estonallie, it became the major shipping point for cotton. When Jackson (Alexandria,) was becoming a settlement, the stage coach would run from Jackson, Denmark, cross the Hatchie at Estonallie, then on to Fayette Corner to Somerville and into Memphis. The earliest maps of West Tennessee show this route. The coach fare was $1.25 from Jackson to Estonallie. As the territory began to develop, steam boats would make the trip from Memphis to Randolph at the mouth of the Hatchie and up to Estonallie. Two hotels were built at Estonallie, Merriwether and McBride. I know this sounds strange to us, but it was a tourist attraction. You could board a gambling boat in Memphis, come up the Mississippi to Randolph, on up to Estonallie and spend the night and go back to Memphis the next day. It was also a major cotton shipping point, cotton buyers would come from Memphis and St. Louis to buy cotton. Madison and Haywood Counties raised some of the finest staples of cotton produced in the U.S. Cotton buyers would came as far away as England to buy this cotton.

Major Joab Wilson was commissioned to build a turn-pike from Denmark to Estonallie and build a bridge across the Hatchie. He already operated a ferry boat there. Jessie James would often camp under some large trees on the banks of the river here. Estonallie was a favorite crossing for Gen. Nathan Bedford Forrest and a camping ground for his troops as well as the Northern Army. Forrest was promoted to Brig. General while camped at Estonallie.

Flat boats could go from Estonallie to Denmark up the Big Black Creek, its banks were kept cleared and you could build a weir to hold back the water until the level would float ad flat boat. The Harbert's brothers had a trading post on the banks of the Big Black Creek, it was the largest in West Tennessee. . Dry goods for the Denmark stores used Big Black as the shipping route.

The steam boats could go on up the Hatchie to **Hatchie Station** and one was built to go all the way up to **Hatchie Town, (Bolivar.)** There was a steam boat turn-around at Hatchie Station. The Pirtle family had a ferry boat at Hatchie Station. It cost five cents to cross the river, and ten cents if you had your horse. . Mr. Pirtle wanted to be buried where he could see the river. He was, but the cemetery flooded so they had to move him

The Hatchie Station Bridge

to higher ground. When the railroad came through it came right along the Hatchie River. There was a large saw mill operation here, logs could be floated down the river to the mill and pushed up into the steam boat turnaround and used when the mill needed them.

There are four Chickasaw Indian mounds on each side of Estonallie. Memphis State under a grant from the Smithsonian is excavating the ones on the Denmark side. The carbon dating is from 1000 AD. The village on the Denmark side had about 500 hundred residents and covered about five acres. Memphis State University is doing the dig with a grant from the Smithsonian. The Smithsonian first discovered the mounds in 1920.

History Of Estaunaula Ferry

(Estonallie, there are many spellings of this name.)

By FONVILLE NEVILLE

Estaunaula meaning in Cherokee language "Here we cross," a onetime ferry on the Hatchie River six miles from Mercer, eight miles from Denmark, has played quite a distinctive part in this section of the country.

A bridge first spanned the river at this point. Its

abandonment was caused by a woman horseman with a small child following behind her falling through it. The Child almost drowned.

Bob Wilson operated the first ferry boat shortly before the War between the States. He built on the bank of the river near the ferry one of the finest homes in the country. Its high ceiling rooms being festooned with marble baskets of flowers; a commodious basement served as kitchen and dining room. Zeno Jones (buried at Ebenezer Cemetery,) from across the river, together with Jim West, father of W T West, constructed the house and there is a legend to the effect that the workmen were promised and given, if they worked swiftly, a quart of whiskey per man per day; but so did grow their thirst with the progress made upon the building before it was finished, they were demanding and receiving a gallon per man each day.

Mr. Wilson owned a large warehouse in which was stored the merchandise brought by the boats from Memphis for merchants mostly at Denmark. He also ran a store. John A Murrell, the infamous "land pirate of the early 1800's often crossed Hatchie river here, the notorious Hearst, Federal commander who preyed on this part of West Tennessee, made the ferry a favorite camping spot. A certain well known dweller of the bottom with strong antipathies against the Yankees had a well secluded tree from the boughs of which he ambushed the Yankees. Whenever buzzards were seen circling low above the brush, the saying went around that "Mr. Jim done got him another dam yank."

A stage road was planned through the bottom from the ferry and was in process of being constructed just prior to the beginning of the War between the States. It would have shortened the distance of travel to Whiteville, Somerville and Memphis. Doctor J. W. Ingram of Denmark was greatly interested in the project and while seeing personally after it, he came down with pneumonia and died in Bob Wilson's home.

Some say it was near the Mississippi line, others say it was near Estaunaula that Egbert Osborne preached his famous sermon from Isaiah, "Son of Man, shall these dry bones live again?" proving to the Yankees by whom he had been captured and taken for a spy and about to be executed, that he was a preacher instead. And not only did he convince them, but he amazed them with his eloquence to the extent he was given a fine horse and safe passage through their lines to go about his theological duties.

A large white oak tree just above the ferry served for several years as a camping spot for one of the Jesse James gang who made a periodical return to the section. He would swim his horse across the river, camp the night under the stars and depart unseen before daybreak.

Tragedy, near tragedy and comedy have run their threads through the history of the old river crossings.

Two brothers, George and Louis Ford, uncles of P. B. Ford, drowned there about sixty years ago. (They are buried in Shady Grove Cemetery, one stone with names on each side.) A ferry boat newly constructed was being launched, it capsized and carried the two men to their death.

There existed no law in those old days regulating the use of the ferry boats; they were improperly fastened to the shore. A family in a new wagon, pulled by oxen drove on the boat. The walking of the oxen moved the boat from shore, and the wagon and its half dozen occupants went into the river.

Fortunately the wagon bed was water tight and floated and was caught and pulled ashore.

There is a legend to the effect that twins about ten years old were drowned there when the ferry boat for some unknown reason sank sometime during the War between the States. They were buried in the old Baptist cemetery in twin graves, brick enclosed.

It was between these graves that $30,000 stolen during the War from a bank in Brownsville, was buried where it remained until about twenty years ago when someone possessing the knowledge of its hiding place dug it up in the dead of the night.

It was at the ferry that a certain prominent member of the County Court performed a bank scaling feat that had no parallel in local history.

He was one of a fishing party, and failing to catch any fish, they had resorted to dynamite. Our 'Squire' tied two sticks together, attached a fuse and tossed aside the river.

So he tried to do.

The strong wind caught it up in a bush not ten feet from the 'Squire where the dynamite, its fuse sputtering angrily, swung back and forth, in a very unsympathetic way.

Behind the 'Squire, blocking his way to safety, was a perpendicular bluff twenty feet high. The frightened

'Squire of hefty proportions, looked at the steadily shortened fuse, cogitated briefly on what two sticks of dynamite would do to his future, and climbed that bluff as if he had the feet of a fly.

Estaunaula, a picturesque name as much so as the Indians who gave it the romantic name, is a link in an Indian trail that ran from the highland of the Ohio to the bluffs of the Mississippi.

The Ford Brothers are buried at Shady Grove Cemetery on Hwy. 223. There is one stone, with the name of the brothers on either side. Estonallie was a favorite crossing during the Civil War, Nathan Bedford Forrest crossed here many time. He was promoted to Brig. General while camped here. When the bridge was built, they would take the planks up and hide them in the woods. Zeno Jones mentioned in this story is buried at Ebenezer Cemetery. Mr. Bob (Joab) Wilson is buried in the Big Black Creek Baptist Cemetery, he had a house in Denmark also. This house was sold to Stephen Carter, and Mr. Stevie Carter was born in it. It would have been on the back street just across the road from the Big Black Creek Baptist Cemetery. The main gate to the cemetery was on this street, the street no longer exists, but you can see the road bed. There are two old corner post still standing. There are cedar tree's here over 100 years old.

* * *

Denmark Merchants from 1847 to 1862

Skillern Brothers Dry Goods

Phillip, Rice, and Cole Lawyers

Phillip, Rice and Gillaspie

Day and Smith General Merchandise

Compton and Skillern Dry Goods

Drake and Henry Lawyers

Tarver and Smith, Doctors

(Doctor Tarver is buried in the Methodist Cemetery)

Neely and Weatherly General Merchandise

Ingram and Skillern

(Ingram was a doctor and died at Estonallie and is buried in Presbyterian Cemetery)

Meriwether and Skillern Salon (doggery)

(The Meriwether owned a hotel also in Denmark and one at Estonallie)

Bevins and Drake, Lawyers

Murchison and Ingram Drug Store

John Wray, Drugs

William Baker, Coffins

(coffin prices varied according to the size of the person, children's coffins were from four to ten dollars.)

Ducker and Wilson Cabinet Shop

Skillern Brothers Boot Shop

(The Stephen Carters ran a tanning business, with as many as 24 workers, it was on the creek bank just past Denmark, it was burnt by the Northern Army)

Mose Brown, Blacksmith

Rainboldt Shop

Weatherly and Sons, General Merchandise

Weatherly Brothers Livery Stables

Henry and Vercer General Merchandise

Harbert Brothers

(The Harbert brothers, John, Stephen and William had the first trading post in West Tennessee on the banks of Big Black Creek, they moved the store to Denmark, it was also the largest trading post in West Tennessee, Bill was the younger brother, he did not marry until he was

35 and he married Mary Waddell , Mary died in Texas and we do not know where. She may have been brought back to Denmark since her family is buried here)

Greenwall and Company

Henry French

(Henry is buried in the Polk/French Cemetery on the 223 just out of Denmark)

Tarver and Detrich

(Dr. Tarver is buried in Methodist Cemetery Denmark)

J. W. McKissack and Company, General Store

Wm. Wilson, Undertaker

(Funerals were priced from about ten dollars up, depending on the service, it they used a horse drawn hearse enclosed it was more)

T. W. Bryan and Company

Skillern and Jackson

Doctor John Tyson

Druggist, Prescriptions Carefully Compounded

Doctor Stack

Doctor Currie

Doctor J. A. Womack

Doctor Newborn

(Dr. Newborn is buried in Methodist Cemetery Denmark)

Newbern & Bro.

Dry Goods, Groceries

Boots, Shoes, Hats, Caps, Notions

Gents Furnishing Goods

Doctor Murdock Murchison

(Dr. Murchison married Fannie Alston he was wounded in the Civil War, and he is buried in Presbyterian Cemetery along with some small children. His son took over the practice. Fannie is buried in the Texas State Cemetery along with the governors of Texas. She out lived all her children) Dr. Murchison attended and graduated from the Philadelphia College of Medicine in 1850-1851 and set up his practice in Denmark. He remained in practice until the start of the Civil War and was mustered into Company D, of the 51st Tennessee Regiment. He was promoted to Captain. His regiment left Corinth, Tennessee and Murchison fought throughout the war and returned to Denmark upon its end.)

J. F. Fonville

Saddlery and Harness

General Repairing Shop

Job Work Solicited

Promptly Attended and

Satisfaction Assured

WM. J Hudson

Maker of Carriages, Wagons and Buggies

General Repair Shop

Whig Tribune 11/29/1870

Improvements: We have a new brick block going up on the corner of Main Street and Carondelet Street…the first of its kind, (all brick,) ever built in this place. It is being built and put by Jeff French (colored) and will be occupied by him as a grocery and restaurant. The extreme high rent forced him to build.

* * *

It is obvious from this list that Denmark was a thriving community. It had three major churches,

Denmark Presbyterian, sometime, considered the Mother Church of Presbyterian Churches in West Tennessee. It was one of the oldest and largest churches in West Tennessee, it had two major schools, a Methodist Church and Big Black Creek Baptist, the largest Baptist Church in West Tennessee at the time, with over 240 members, not counting the slaves. The West Tennessee Baptist Association was formed here.

* * *

Stephen Carter

The Stephen Carter family has always played a major role in the life of Denmark. He had married Eliza Rosser Carter when he was 19 and she was 16. They came to West Tennessee in 1845. Stephen had learned the tanner's trade from his oldest brother, Billy in North Carolina so he established a small tannery and did reasonably well along with working a small farm they had acquired and also did some carpentry. He also made furniture, it shows the Quaker influence he grew up with.

They came to Medon, TN. first. They were members of the Clover Creek Baptist Church where they buried three children. *The current Clover Breek Baptist is not at the original site of the Church, it is just out of Medon and the original cemetery is at that site. Some of the earliest settlers of Madison County are buried there.* In 1855 they acquired 54 acres in Denmark, with excellent advantages for a fine tannery. This property was at the foot of a hill where a sand branch runs. Water was necessary for the processing of raw material into leather.

The Denmark Community was a prosperous community with an increasing demand for good leather and manufactured articles, harnesses, saddles, bridles, boots and shoes. In a few years there were seven buildings, two large sheds and 25 or more good workmen.

The Civil War however was undoing all over the South, the prospects of many good and industrious people. Denmark was occupied at different times by both Confederate and Federal Forces.

In the later part of the war a detachment of Cavalry in passing halted in front of the tan yard and command was given to light the fire which burned to the ground the entire operation. It was a total loss.

Of eleven children, six survived to adulthood, one son and five daughters.

Denmark Elementary School

Mr. Stevie Carter became a mail carrier and acquired a very large farm priding himself as a great cotton farmer. The Carter's are buried in the Denmark Presbyterian Cemetery. They were active members of the Big Black Creek Baptist Church until it closed.

* * *

Fire Camps on Town's Trail

By Fonville Neville

Denmark, Tenn. Aug 30, A fiery nemesis has pursued the little village of Denmark, the oldest town in West Tennessee, almost to its doom. Since a day in 1863 when a chance spark ignited a pile of shavings in the rear of Wilson and Ducker's cabinet shop, fires have played a large part in the decadence of the once prosperous village. This fire was to largest consuming 17 business houses and a number of smaller shops.

On Tuesday night the first day of May, 1867, in the

The Rosser Family with their slaves
One Mule and two Horses

shoe shop of negro, Jerry Meriwether, another fire broke out, which again destroyed almost the entire business district.

In July 1906 another fire occurred, starting in the store of Reid and McKisseck, which also was the post office. Three business houses burned. Since then four gins have burned, one destroying by the bursting of the boiler and 14 dwellings and only two of them were replaced. In one of the fires an aged negress burned to death.

Other serious fires have been narrowly averted. When the old Henry place burned this spring, the Presbyterian Church nearby barely escaped, owing to the difficulty of the flames in reaching its roof. A large building and one of the oldest in the country, if it had caught the entire village would have been in danger. Last summer when the old Williamson place went up in smoke, the entire western portion of the village was endangered. The Presbyterian mance and the Burton place both caught as did a barn. Zealous work by volunteer firemen saved the day.

For more than 75 years, the large bell in the Presbyterian church yard has pealed out the alarms. The last fire here was in the home of M. Barnes two weeks ago. Barring a few negro cabins on the outskirts there are only 14 homes left. Just a few more years, it seems, are all the fiery nemesis will need to write finis to the history of one of the first of West Tennessee's towns.

* * *

Battle of Britton's Lane Was Fought for High Ideals

By FONVILLE NEVILLE (Denmark Historian)

The only thing agreed upon by all sources about the fight at Britton's Lane was the number of Federals captured-213.

Three "Rebs" surrendered, presumably prisoners. But there was opinion they deserted.

It was not uncommon to err in those days, the modes of communication primitive and difficult. even the Jackson Daily Blade, a Memorial Edition dated

The Bell at the Denmark Presbyterian Church is silver. It was cast from silver of the ladies of the town. It was cast in Philadelphia, PA. Each of the three Churches in Denmark had a bell, the Baptist and Methodist were in their bell towers, but the Denmark Presbyterian Bell was to heavy. It was used for many purposes, Church services, funerals, fire and to call the town together. It can be heard for eight miles. They rang it 150 time at the celebration of the building of the Church , built in 1854. It also rang when the Denmark Danes left for the Civil War and for their funerals when the bodies were brought home. .

Wednesday, May 15, 1895, set the battle up four months, stating it took place at 11 a.m. May 3, 1862.

J. B. Young in his history of 7th Tenn. Cavalry puts the Confederates killed at 13 with 55 wounded. Billy Witherspoon said the general estimate of killed and wounded in the 7th was not more than 10 or 12 killed and about the same number wounded. A Capt. McNeil, who had been the leader in erecting the monument, said at the day of its placing that Billy was wrong. From his investigation and corresponding with the different regiments engaged, "Our loss in killed and wounded was near 115."

This estimate, of course, included the casualties of all the regiments engaged.

Pending the erection of the monument that now stands, the field of Britton's Lane was curried for the bones of the fallen soldiers buried where they had fallen by Jim Lewis Collins, his brother George and others and those found were placed in the trench over which the monument stands.

If this writer's memory does not play him false- he was on the ground the day the monument was dedicated - he was told the trench contained the bones of 21 men.

However, Mr. Collin's estimate is more than that.

Three of the killed were brought to the Presbyterian Cemetery at Denmark and buried: Dr. Joe Allen of Whiteville, Ed Peters, father of a former Methodist minister at the Methodist Church here, and a young boy of an Alabama regiment whose identity remained a secret until many years after the war.

It is no fresh truth to say men become inured to death, its gruesome preface and aftermath, and yet (so William [Bill] Henry who, aided by a Negro Shedrick Pipkins, performed the interment of the three) told afterwards there was something about that fresh young boy's body, his casket a coarse woolen blanket, that made the shoveling of dirt upon it a profanation he never forgot and always remembered with pity.

The boy was not over 15 years old, clad in a homemade uniform on which had been sewed buttons of strange military design. For this fact, coupled with pity that the lad should sleep out time in a forgotten and unmarked grave, Henry cut off one of the buttons which later he gave to Capt. Guthrie telling him where it came from.

A teacher of men and also a student of them, Capt. Guthrie knowing like John Hubbard the unaccountable things of not only war but of events carried the button to every reunion he attended.

It was the custom of Confederate reunions for homes in the cities to be opened to the old soldiers who had worn the Grey. In Atlanta Mrs. Jefferson made her home welcome to them and it was one of those unaccountable things that every soldier who was housed in the old mansion had ridden with Forrest.

To say one rode with Forrest was open season to any home.

Talk as usual about the table was of the war. Mrs. Jefferson's husband killed at First Manassas; her young son just turned 14 ran away to join Forrest which was the reason, she stated, she felt she was one of the gathering.

He had written her, her reminiscences ran on, from Corinth, Miss. Needing clothes badly. She had made him a uniform from the one worn by his great-grandfather at Yorktown with George Washington, mailed it to him and never heard from him again.

She had waited and hoped after the war that perhaps he would come straggling home. Then, as he had not, had grieved that he slept on some field in an unknown and unmarked grave.

With the strange feeling of prescience Capt. Guthrie had produced the button cut from the homemade uniform of a boy soldier who had died on Britton's Lane.

Doubtless there had been similar buttons sown on homemade uniforms at that period. But some strands of the thread Mrs. Jefferson had used had clung to the button and those she identified as the thread she had used in sewing on the buttons of the Continental uniform Sanderson Jefferson's great-grandfather had worn on the uniform she had cut down for her son.

So the bones of the young soldier who had died in the arms of Aunt "Mog", heroine of Britton's Lane, instead of being in a common trench beneath a generalizing commemorative stone came to rest finally beside the venerated bones of his grandshire who had died at Yorktown.

The only effect of the small affair of arms at Britton's Lane was the disheartening effect on the Confederates engaged in the fight.

Billy Witherspoon in his reminiscence goes on to say the Federals were whipped several times in the fight and as many time hoisted the white flag… "Why having that battlefield in less than 10 minutes after artillery was captured and not a gun fired or any demonstration of the enemy to recapture it…"

Billy Witherspoon must have meant victory was very evident which they had not recognized… "When in fact, as told by a citizen of Denmark, over 200 of the Yankees returned there and were anxious to find someone to surrender to"… Believing they were whipped ¯ "We were certainly on the run to say the least, a forced march, nor halting nor stopping until we were ferried across the Hatchie, 16 miles distant, on a ferry boat."

Billy also told of one of the captured guns being so badly damaged it could not be moved farther and was thrown down an old dug well.

Jim Miller, who lived across the ravine from the place of battle several miles, said as a boy he distinctly remembered seeing half buried in the sand of the creek that flowed through the ravine the brass barrel of a small cannon…

But if one man, 10 or 1,000 died at Britton's Lane it is hallowed ground.

It is where men struggled, bled and died not for greed nor fame, not even in anger, but for a principle, an ideal, each thought was right.

Although that principle or ideal today has come to assume debatable hues, it is to be honored and observed and preserved, because men were willing to fight for it, to die for it in the conviction they were right.

"The muffled drum's sad roll has beat
The soldier's last tattoo!
No more on life's parade shall meet
The brave and fallen few.

"On Fame's eternal camping ground
Their silent tents are spread,
And glory guards with solemn round
The bivouac of the dead."

* * *

The Denmark Danes

I have often wondered where all the Denmark Danes are buried, we have a few in our local cemeteries, but many are missing. We know that they were at Shiloh in several battles. We think over half of them were killed there. When I found this article I wondered if many are not still at Shiloh.

Jackson Tribune and Sun. Vol. I, No. 22, Nov. 23, 1877 Jackson, TN

CONFEDERATE DEAD ASSOCIATION—Your committee appointed to visit the battlefield and report the condition of the remains of the Confederate dead, respectfully submit the following: The remains of the Confederate dead, who fell in battle on the 5th and 6th days of April, 1862, lie scattered over an area of about fifteen square miles, on the hills , and in the valleys. Near Mr. PUNT's house, where there were some white posts put up by the federals, are two large piles and several smaller ones, supposed to contain about 300 said to be troops from Texas. Many of these ghastly relics are exposed to the light of the sun, the wind and the rain, bleaching under the influence of the elements. In the direction of Fort Wallace, by several settlements, are many scattering pits and graves. Many remains are lying on the ground where they were covered with a few shovels of dirt, no graves or pits being dug. Around Henry BARLEY"S premises are many remains, some in pits and others in single graves. Many of these are exposed, besides many scattered through the woods and fields, around the old church grounds, for a mile or two. (We know the

Danes were in this area.) A great many remains are in pits and graves and in gullies. Many of these are exposed and lie in heaps, mingled with dirt and rubbish, undistinguished and undistinguishable. Many of these are exposed, some washed off by the rains, others rooted by hogs and some never covered at all, or so imperfectly as to be easily washed off by rain and left exposed to the actions of the elements. From Mr. HOUSE's to Mr. D. S. MICHIE's about four miles west are many graves scattered on both sides of what is known as the old Bark Road. Some of these although covered from sight, yet there are many bones scattered over the hills and hollows and lying in the woods exposed. Your committee thinks and believe that about 1,000 remains can be easily found and gathered up. Many, of course cannot be found, after the long lapse of 15 years, it would hardly be possible under the circumstances of mutation and change that have taken place on the battle grounds. Committee: J. M. MITCHELL: N.S.ATKINS, C.C. STEEL, DR.. THORNTON, W. J. SUTTON.

* * *

Sun Forum

I hate change of any sort with all the intensity of the proverbial Britisher, not that it affects in any material way my private life, but in some subtle way affects the facets of the world that I live in.

There are changes that affect my spiritual world; more specifically, there are changes that change the very atmosphere of things one had lived with so long.

This is the reason that I regret to hear of David Murray's impending retirement from the office of district attorney.

For as long as I can remember, and my memory runs back to many cycles of Jackson and Madison County history, Baltimore Street had proclaimed the domain of the Murrays, and the street will not be the same without the sign of Murray inhabiting the door of an office ⎯ unpretentious as that door seems before it gathered both the common people and the notables of West Tennessee and all found a mutual welcome.

It has been a door plain enough in its design but very significant of the personality that has given it the dignity and warm friendship that have existed so long behind it, not to mention the talent that had also added more luster to the name of Murray.

Fonville Neville

Denmark

* * *

LEIGHTON COMMUNITY

A small community sprang up at a cross roads of the Denmark/Woodland Road. We are not sure where the name came from, there are no Leighton's in the history of the community. At first there was a store and cotton gin built here. Arthur Curlin and some of his brothers owned the store. They were the sons of Isach Washington Curlin. Arthur had married Elvira Witherspoon. The community had built a small two room school here called Booker Knob, we don't know where that name came from either, the only record we have is in Maggie Dickinson's Bible. She says "all my children went to Booker Knob School.". Elivra had come to teach at the school which was just down the road from Curlin and Curlin Store. Elvira boarded with the Valentine family just down the road from the school. Arthur and Elvira married. They bought a farm and built a house at Leighton. Earnest Dickinson and his brother John Dickinson set up a black smith shop and grist mill across from the store. The Curlins opened a cotton gin, which was later sold to L. M. Wilson. Harvey Print and his wife Hannah Dickinson Curlin built a house on the corner across from the store. Richard Spencer and Rosa Dickinson King lived across the Denmark Road and Spence worked in the black smith shop with his brothers–in-laws. Spence was also a share cropper for Mr. Harbert Rice. Later the Kings bought the Valentine Farm just down the road from Leighton. John and Mary Dickinson Dickinson lived just down the road with their children, John died young of TB and left Miss Mary to raise the children, she taught piano. There was a post office in the Curlin Store, using a Leighton address.

There is a sad part of this story. If you are a farmer you will understand this term, the country stores would "run" the farmers until their crops came in. Meaning they would supply them with seeds, food, and clothing until they could sell their crops. Curlins Store did this for the local farmers. When the depression hit, the farmers could not pay and Arthur lost the store, his farm and home during the depression. L. M. Wilson bought the gin, West bought the store and Nona Dickinson Childress bought the farm. But, there is a ending, remember Elvira was a Whitherspoon, and her uncle gave them a place to live. When he died he left them his farms in Madison County which were thousands of acres. They had four children, Martha, Mildred, Hewett and Billy who died very young. Martha lived to be 98, and married twice, Mildred was killed in the store they owned on the Harts Bridge Road, Hewitt died as a result of a car accident. He was in his late 80's. They are all buried in the Woodland Cemetery in Haywood County. None of them had children.

Leighton had one murder, Mr. Dickinson was sitting in his parlor reading his Bible when a disgruntled worker shot and killed him, his wife Sadie and small child were in the house. They are buried in the Woodland Cemetery.

In and around Leighton there were several other families, Yelverton, Wilson, West, Bond, Dickinson, Rice, Boggs, Hudson, Forrest, and Dr. John Norvell.

* * *

**EARNEST AND VEVA KING DICKINSON
MR EARNEST OPERATED THE BLACK SMITH SHOP AND GRIST MILL
AT LEIGHTON**

The Forrest family were brick masons, they had two kilts one was just across from the Dickinson farm where they had found a red clay bank to make the bricks. Most of our old buildings have Forrest bricks in them.

* * *

John J. Dickinson homestead was located on the north side of the present County Line road/Woodland Church Road, which largely follows the route of the old Brownsville-Denmark road of the previous century. It was on a hill across the road from the Forrest Place. The farm extended into both counties, with the house on the line. John J's son, John Clint must have enjoyed that, because his children remember his saying many times that he grew up eating in Madison County and sleeping in Haywood County without leaving home. The John J. Dickinson farmland was a part of the original Samuel Brown tract. Some of it he bought from his wife's sister when the Brown Estate was settled, and part of it came into his possession upon the death of his wife, Anna Arabella Brown (Annie), daughter of Samuel Brown. At age 32, Annie died leaving John J. with five children ages two to eleven. He soon married a young

The Dickinson Family of Leighton ,Tennessee. This house is just over in
Haywood County, it actually straddled the county line of Madison and Haywood
Counties. Mr. John Dickinson would say he slept in Madison County and ate in
Haywood. In 1903 they bought the Dawson Bond farm and moved on what is now
Hwy. 138 at Leighton. From left to right is Earnest Dickinson the oldest child,
then John, Mr. Dickinson, Mrs. Maggie Dickinson with Rosa in her lap, the
youngest child at the time, Nona, and Hannah. Later they had two more children,
Clint and Robert. The farm is still in the Dickinson Family.

widow, Rebecca Stokley Clark, who had three little boys. John and Rebecca added five more children of their own, become a family of 15 plus one or two hands who lived with them to help with the work. L Put another way, that means 51 plates to be filled and 17 outfits of clothes to wash. Rebecca Dickinson was a strong and valiant lady! The Dickinson children found mates in neighboring families such as Musgrave, Hudson, Mann, Curlin, Wilson and even other Dickinson's. their families worshiped at Brown's Creek Missionary Baptist Church (now Woodland Baptist Church). Many of them still have still have descendants living in the Woodland Church area today. *Complied by Mrs. Virginia Dickinson.* .

John Clint Dickinson Sr. had a 600 acre track of land at Leighton which he had bought from the Dawson Bond Estate. He and Margaret Glass Dickinson had, seven children, Hannah, Earnest, Nona, John, Clint, Rosa and Robert. They had lost their house on the Woodland Road to fire. They bought the Bond farm in 1903. The home place house had burnt down. They had been picking cotton and saving some in cotton baskets for quilting, putting it upstairs. While John was shaving early in the morning he noticed that the cotton was on fire. They put

the fire out and went to the cotton field only to look back and the house was on fire. They managed to save only three pieces of furniture. They had to borrow clothes from relatives until they could make more, they had just remodeled the house and had pulled the old kitchen away from the house. John , Maggie and the girls moved into the old kitchen. The boys sleep in the loft of the barn. It is at this point they bought the old Dawson Bond farm on what is now Hwy. 138 in Leighton. This farm is still in the family.

Mrs. Maggie was a very industrious woman, she raised capons (castrated roosters, they grew very large and the meat was very tender, better than turkey) and sold them at the farmers market in Jackson. She also had large flower gardens where she raised all types of flowers, she sold to the Jackson florist. For many years she saw that fresh flowers were always in the Woodland Church every Sunday. Clint, the youngest daughter played the piano for Woodland, and later Mrs. Maggie's grandson, John Dickinson Jr. lead the music at the Church. He went to Union and a Baptist Seminary and became the Minister of Music at First Baptist Church in Lake Charles, LA. Her great grandson is Billy King. (she was the first person I saw die, I was sitting on the side of her bed at 10 years old when she died.) Three of her children died of TB, John, Clint and Robert. She had sent Clint and Robert to New Mexico for treatment. John died in a little house that was in the front of the house, with windows all around it so he could see his children playing in the yard. All of the family, but Robert, are buried at Woodland. Robert had married and his wife buried him at Hollywood. He sold cars for Truex, and always drove a new car.....his nephews called him a "dude."

This house on the old Bond farm was hit by a tornado and was destroyed all but a log room, it was given to Big Back Creek and has been rebuilt on Hwy.138 and Ebenezer Road.

In 1940, Margaret Glass Dickinson and her children signed a easement with TVA bringing the first electric power to the community. The old house was lite by gas and the fixtures were still there (not in use,) when the tornado hit the house.

* * *

What Happened To Southern Courtesy?

In the old days it was both an index to character and how one was raised. Today it has ceased to be.

Among us who have passed the meridian of life, there still lingers a mother's admonition against thoughtfulness: "Did you wipe your feet, sonny boy?" If one hadn't, there followed an accusation one could not forget, "You must have been raised in a barn."

I am brought to exclaim upon this by a housewife, who had been absent from home several days and returned to find her new rug, she had left shining and clean, mud-and-dust spattered by the young persons who had visited her daughter.

She had cried in some indignation , "I don't see why people can't pause long enough to wipe their feet at the door".

Why had that custom been disregarded? For one thing, because of stone pavements and roads, automobiles.

More, I believe, can be charged to lack of training, the absence of old Southern culture, and the disinterest in good manners. That had been submerged by crass individualism of time, due to the rush, the bustle, the drive to fame and fortune, the defense of a mode of living that one gets there first.

I am minded to use as an example the care of one of the most proud, vain and arrogant queens of Europe, Queen Marie Antoinette of France.

When she was being led up the steps to the guillotine where she was to meet death, she accidentally trod on the foot of one of the brutal guards, who was aiding her.

"Watch where you are walking, you hussy," he snarled at the Queen of France.

And the Queen of France responded, "I am sorry. Please forgive me."

Fonville NeVille

Denmark

* * *

Fisherman's Luck

By FONVILLE NEVILLE

He never got in a hurry, this fisherman we knew. He took good luck and bad luck in his stride, his speech was slow̄ easy: his dress a bit careless and rough; his habits regular, a sort of routine that seldom varied and which made him a part of our life like the days and nights.

There was always in his reservoir of memory a quaint and humorous tale with a philosophical twist. To his piscatorial skill were added other arts, commonplace but necessary to our wellbeing.

To round his character he mellowed now and then with a bit of the stuff all good fishermen carry as a condiment to their calling and which brought to the surface a Fallstaffian geniality.

Like all of this kind, he did all things unobtrusively and well, the best he knew how̄ with the sureness of one whose path day after day would be unaltered by any degree save by such powers as he could not control. His many hours of solitude beside quiet pools in the shade of friendly trees which to aim had tongues made him a votary of the little and sweet things of life; not for him were there temples of Mammon, places and citadels of fame and success but true contentment and quiet happiness. True for him there were "sermons in stones, books in brooks and good in everything."

The atmosphere of his chosen avocation was continually about him. When he shouldered rod or gun there shadowed him and spoke to the onlookers' imagination all the ancestry and a bit of likeness of Rip Van Winkle himself.

He scoffed at signs such as men of science put in almanacs; the zodiac chart could not be read by fish, he said; some innate instinct spoke to him when and where. He could follow the most skilled Waltonite of us and catch double our scare.

"Oh, I don't know," he would say with his slow mile. "Fish will bite when they're hungry regardless if the sign is in their tail or mouth. If they are not hungry; well fisherman's luck," he'd say with a twinkle in his eyes.

He has tramped down the old road for the last time; the leafy bowers which he alone knew will welcome him no more; the shadowed dappled pools will not reflect his image again, nor ripple to the casting of his hook; the little paths which wended their silent way through thicket and wood to favored haunts will not echo his quiet step hereafter.

Only the memory of his quiet, undeviating way, his quaint philosophy and a picture of him in the sun is our hereafter; his slow moving familiar figure had withdrawn into deeper shadows, where quiet pools and shady nooks await him, deeper than the eye can pierce.

The accustomed bench outside the box against the wall will send others who still chase their phantoms, yet the shadow of him will linger over them ̄ the shade of one who with rod or gun or sorrow or joy, asked only of life "Fisherman's luck!"

* * *

The Overturned Mailbox

My rural mail route goes through a backwoods section where happiness is a rare commodity. Once a year the highway department cleans out the roadside ditches, upsetting some of the mailboxes. Since it's against rules to dump mail on the ground, I have to stop and blow my horn at the homes of the folks who haven't put their boxes back up.

At one home one year, a youngster always ran out

to get the mail. :Bet you won't have to blow your horn tomorrow," he'd say, and each day it became a game to see whether I'd get there before he did.

Meanwhile, his dad kept promising to replace the mailbox, but never did. Finally, I gave notice that mail would have to be discontinued.

Next morning he met me, "Mister," he said, "Sammy gets a lot of fun out of your visits. It's the best thing he likes. Every morning he gets up and talks about meeting you before you blow your horn. So if I put up that mailbox…"

"Skip it," I said.

Sammy's still racing to beat the horn.

F. Neville, Denmark, Tenn.

The story of Mr. Fonville and his mail route is a great one. It is said you could set your clock by his run, every day he would be at your house at the same time. He always watched out for everyone on his route and would often stop to see if they were alright. Mr. Fonville knew everyone on his route personally. He was not just the mail man he was their friend.

To An Old Friend

By FONVILLE NEVILLE

Why grieve over some hopeless flaw

In stone tablets of the law,

When Scriptures every day afresh

Is engraved on tablets of the flesh.

We thought of these words by a great poet as we listened to the preacher.

They placed her in the earth beneath the benediction of a gentle sky, laved by the soft glow of the sinking sun; invisible hands of the wind rustled the dead leaves of the overhanging trees. They made a sad undertone for the dull sound of the clods, a muffled sob, the preacher's voice, "Ashes to ashes, dust to dust."

Aye, blessed she was resting in the mellowness of humanity's service, rooted in unselfish love! Surely her sleep will be gentle and deep…

The present generation, of which one, well past

mature years is in a sense a bystander, views its generation as a golden one, filled and overflowing like a horn of cornucopia with the utmost skills of science, and which promises to bring to birth those yet more glorious. Notwithstanding it is more or less a mechanized generation and a superficial one which had grown away from the simple, natural things. It snatches at the gilded froth and lets the substance go.

Yesterday we looked upon a scene that is writing the final chapter of an era which we would like to call the richest phase of life as we knew it. As the dirt fell upon the coffin we sensed that it was not only covering a body but a generation, the like of which will never be seen again. It marked the passing one by one of the old time Negro: the black "mammies" and "uncles" and "aunts" of our childhood.

A Northerner once said about social equality, why should we object to it? We claim kin with the Negro. We call them "Uncle" and "Aunt." But if that poor fellow only knew the real significance of these terms, the association which went into their birth, he would read in them a deeper kinship than blood. Incomprehensible as it might seem to him it is a kinship of love.

Do we find in the fair young face of our childhoods,

resting in perfect security against a black bosom a thought of equality save the equality of love and faith; in the black wrinkled face bending above us so tenderly and solicitous any dream of equality? The bond which grew out of this was greater than equality. In all the orbit of human relationship there exist no parallel to the loyalty which bound the old time Negro to his white folks that in turn exacted a loyalty which transcended color.

It was rooted in serfdom. From the black mammy who crooned a lullaby and rocked her little white lamb to sleep, her charge of it, her love for it, her very life for it; deep into the babes inner self flowed these things to start a tide that ran unthinned down the years, generation after generation.

The slave who guarded the southern homes with a love and trust he held above freedom; the one who followed his young master into battle, searching bloody fields for him to gather him in his arms and to bring him home to die. Such a tide could not cease to flow until its channels withered.

And this no doubt is the reason that in all history no other two races so different in color, temperament and ancestry have lived together in such a state of harmony.

Our earliest infancy was centered about a turbaned, wrinkled black face whose love and patience ran through the longest days; her arms a sanctuary against all ills and fears, whose voice, poetical in resonance, crooned us to sleep, in light, watched the leaping flames as she told us of Brier Rabbit and Brier Fox. Who had pet names for such, names which had a hundreds variations of the great note that has stirred the pulse of the world since time began the note of love. And with her the others were linked. There, we came to know was no bottom to their loyalty, no barriers that they would not cross, nor depths to which they would not descend to lift us up. High might have grown our station, mighty our name, or soiled and ragged our state, we never exceeded the bounds of their heads were crowned with silver we venerated them. We honored them with endearing names...

As the preacher talked we seemed to hear a soft voice in our ear feel a hand on the head of our childhood with the gentleness if a prayer. Such we will not hear nor feel again. A great sadness fell on us.

So the generation, of which she was a part and is no more, passes. Not with a magnificent glitter or pageantry but in an aura of gentleness, patience, faith, and love and loyalty, so kindred and great a group as to give it pomp and power, not equaled in the past not to be excelled in the future, it mists the eyes, tightened the throat and wrings a sob from the heart. And leave a glow and a song against the sky!

We, as "Sonny" salute you. "Aunt" Francis! The faithful friend of our gathering years, the second mother of our youth. May you sleep well after life's fitful fever. Your body will mold to dust, but no dust will gather on our memory of you and your kind!

* * *

My two mammies Bill King

I remember with great fondness the two black ladies who helped raise me; Minnie Butler was in the house when I was born and for many years helped care for me and Nell Waddle, who also played a great part in my early life. Many years later after Nell's husband died, we moved her to town so she could go to work at the hospital and build up some Social Security. She would not ride a taxi nor city bus, so I had to take her back and forth to my house and work. One day I got very upset with her because she keep calling me to come take her home. When I got to the house to get her, I told her if she ever did that again, she could not come to my house again. She was a little frail woman and I am six foot three...she taped me on the shoulder and said, "Let me tell you something white boy, I will come to your house when I get ready, and there is nothing you can do about it."

Minnie is still living in Bemis and the street she lives is named for her, Butler, she will be 99 in 2013. Her husband Willis was my grandfather's right hand man. Just before my grandfather died he wanted to go see Willie, they sat in the car for hours laughing and telling stories, when we got ready to leave, my grandfather said to Willie, "I won't see you again Willie." I did not realize that he was telling Willie good bye. When my grandfather died in 1975, he was 85, I called Minnie to tell her, she first decided that we would not tell Willie that "Mr. Spence" had died. Willie was very sick and in a wheel chair from a stroke. But, Minnie called me back and said, "Bill I have to tell Willie, because he ask about Mr. Spence every day." I asked if she wanted me to come get them, but she said no, I will get someone to bring us, just meet us at the door of the funeral home. Blacks did not come to white funeral homes much in 1975. I waited for them and we got Willie out of the car and took him into the chapel where my grandfather was. I rolled Willie down next to the coffin, he did not say a word for a long time, then he reached over in the casket and patted my grandfather on the hand and said, "I will see you in Heaven Mr. Spence." There was not a dry eye in the funeral home. Willie did not live much longer after that. They were true friend to the end, now they are having a great time in heaven planting cotton and bailing hay. Some friends are forever.

* * *

Along Rural By-Paths (A Sunday Gathering)

By FONVILLE NEVILLE

They gathered last Sunday-the fourth Sunday in August-on the third anniversary of home coming day at old Ebenezer-G. G. Pope and wife, Mrs. Sallie Mai Hensley and son, Pharis; M. C. Mulheron, Miss Ruth Mulheron, Fenner Pope and wife, Mr. and Mrs. Ross

McCauley, Charlie Glenn and family, Charlie Rainey, Mr. and Mrs. Francis Wold and daughter, Mrs. Mary Dickinson and children, Dorothy Pope, Lewis Byran and wife, Mrs. Ala Beard, Mrs. Mary Bond, Emory Batchelor, Mr. and Mrs. Bill Christopher, Mrs. Lula Pope, Miss Nyta Mulheron, Mr. and Mrs. Albert Mulheron, Miss Anna and Mary Strayhorn, John Strayhorn and wife, Mrs. Lizzie Walters, Mrs. Julia Rutledge, Mrs. Fonville Neville, Katherine Neville, Mrs. Mai Jane Stewart, Jimmie Mullins, Dave Murray and mother, Mrs. Dick Neely, Mrs. Willie Malhart and son, Mr. and Mrs. John Goodwin and visitor, Mr. and Mrs. Carl Ward, Mr. and Mrs. Neely Mayo, Miss Mamie Rose, Jim Midgett, wife and son, Miss Thomas, Mrs. Dave Givens, Mrs. N. T. Pentecost, Miss Christine Kelly and sister, Mr. and Mrs. M. C. Pope and daughter, Miss Hunt–in whose lives the old church had played directly or indirectly an important part; some as members, some whose parents have worshipped there and others to pay homage to its historic and sacred memories.

Churches are built today-immense piles of brick and stone creations of a genius' brain, fashioned by a master craftsman, rearing their spires to the clouds.

They inspire admiration, invoke wonder and awe, but in their pomp and grandeur defeat the purpose for which they were erected. They bring no sentiment to the human heart; they fill no soul with the benediction of hope and faith. Imperial thrones, tabernacles of majesty, they speak to the heart in crass materialism rather than spiritual beauty; symbols of worship of the great and mighty but not of love of mercy. They entice the rich but drive the poor away.

A certain church not so long ago celebrated the completion of an annex. Ministries of the city were invited to participate. The presiding elder preached the dedicatory sermon. Beautiful flowers and congratulatory messages came from many sources. The pastor spoke of the money involved-a good many thousands of dollars and the presiding elder congratulated the members for their fine cooperation.

Not a stone's throw from that church live people who have never been invited within its doors. Across the street is a young couple whose home the pastor had never entered, and whose lone invitation to attend the services came from the young woman's former school teacher.

Apparently forgotten the Christly metaphor-"I was a stranger and you took me in."

"Or is it you who boast of light, Claim yet a too

exclusive right?"

But the old church! Whether in the vale on hill or in the wild wood, knew no strangers and all who came within its doors were blessed!

No imposing structure to crush one's trembling hope, to drive one's faith in awe to the dust by the thunder of its munificence, and one from the portals by the alikeness of pomp and creed-pride exalted, piety forgotten!

It had no stained windows dedicated to some departed soul; no spires pointing vaingloriously, a sepulcher of hopes but a temple of ostentation. Not to capitalize God but to honor Him, a shrine and sanctuary, inspirational of hope and peace; where father and mother had worshipped, aye, even where their father and mother had worshipped, and hallowed for that. Sacred to the memories of those known for their piety and worth, consecrated by their faith and dear to the living for this dedication.

Where stands an old church is the heart strings of a people. The feet that trod its aisles, the forms which filled the pews, the figures the rostrum held bring a grace and benediction upon it far beyond marital powers to do.

As one in reverence treads softly down the old, old aisle it becomes memory peopled of the long ago.

Mother sat here. One can see her in the soft light, dim and golden cast, and the sweet serenity of faith which sat upon her brow gave to it and to her a light not of earth. Erect, this dear little mother of one whose loved ones fully had found in expendable in the majesty of God! And what beauty of stone, wealth of metal could enhance the value of that crude bench on which she sat?

There in the "amen" corner was father's seat-there by the wondow. How clearly one can see his grey, bent head; how well remembered the shaft of sunlight that often struck upon his upturned face benediction ally, as with closed eyes he supplicated Heaven in simple words for the need of the crudest there.

One touches the back of the bench where his trembling hands had clasped as one would touch the hand of God Himself.

And as one stands in reverse, out of the years comes the figures that have graced the pulpit, dignitaries not by a whole alphabet after their names but in their own right. The glory of their services shines about them; the duties of office faithfully done.

The marriages. That happiness done there. The tenderness of the solace when death came. The baptismal rites when through them flowed the grace of the Master, and the crowning glory of turning wayward feet homeward.

To the memory of each clings tender, individual incidents.

Even the grounds have their share of memories. At the foot of "yonder nodding beech" the first love was declared, the first sweet kiss given. Sad eyes that maybe looked a moment before upon a grass grown mound grows bright with tears of happy memory.

"There's the limbs dad used to hitch the horses to, and here's where he always stopped the wagon. Remember the hornet's nest we got into?... "Right over there is where Uncle Jack Bryan tied his horse, never missing a step rain or shine.

So with the old Ebenezer Cumberland Presbyterian Church, over a century old, in all that span, having but two pastors Parson Joe Pope, and he was beloved known, father of G. G. Pope, the oldest living member, and Wm. Norment, called in the same terms of affection "Uncle Norment." He died only a few years ago, ninety seven years old.

A direct descendent of the first pastor Lee Pop Ward of Jackson is present filling the pulpit of the church now moved to Mercer in a recently erected building.

He preached that morning at the old church, dinner was served, the afternoon spent in recalling the old days and singing old songs. Then home.

And old Ebenezer thought dead, still lives.

In 1910 the Ebenezer congregation bought land in Mercer, Tn. and built a new church building. It has two towers one taller than the other, the taller is over the men's door and the short one is the women's and children's door. The church is the property of The Big Black Creek Historical Association and has been restored. There are three cemeteries at the old site on Ebenezer Road, two black and one white. The slaves are in one, they were members of the Church, Allen and Diecy Norman were freed slaves who had gotten a land grant and came from North Carolina with a mule, cow and wagon. The land is still in the Norman family. Allen was very active in the Ebenezer Church. I have reason to believe that during a great revival at the Church, the song writer Bliss led the music and wrote the old hymn,

"Whosoever Will May Come."

The church had pews on the left and right sides facing the pulpit, the two on the right were for the elders, deacons of the church, often referred to as the "amen" corner. The widows of the church sat on the two on the left side of the building. Often referred to as "Mothers of the Church." In some of the churches men sit on one side while women and children on the other. The old Church had a pot belly stove right in the middle, we left the old stove pipe.

* * *

On July 2nd, 1888, T. E. Mercer and F. M. McGlathery filed their statement presented in words that caused the town of Mercer to be planned and surveyed within the region of the "Big Black Creek," and the Tennessee Midland Railway. In 1889 building lots were being sold. W. S. Nuckolls, L. W. McGee, M. J. Siler, Louis H. Lowenstein and E. D. Bond were among the first Grantees of Land in Mercer by Grantor T. E. Mercer. There was already a stage road which crossed the Tennessee Midland Railroad and a log cabin belonging to Eaton Bond. The Eaton Bond log house was where the McGlathery House now stands, and some of the logs were used for the seals of this house. Eaton and his brother Dawson were squatters before the Treaty with the Chickasaw was signed in 1818. The Dawson Bond cabin has been restored and is at Ebenezer Road and U. S. Hwy. 138.

Mr. Mercer was coming down the Big Black Creek from Denmark and he got to the place where the new railroad was being laid out. He went back to Toone, Tennessee, where he had a general store with his son and son-in-law, Mr. Franklin McGlathery and told them this was a perfect place for a town. It had the new railroad, the Big Black Creek where flatboats were going up to Denmark was and about four miles from the Estonallie Landing on the Hatchie River. The Hatchie at that time was a major trade route with steam boats coming up from Memphis and St. Louis almost on daily trips. Mr. Franklin went over and bought the land and built the first store building. He had married Mattie Mercer; they lived upstairs over the new store. A railroad station was then built and Mr. Franklin became the station master. He built the first house in Mercer in 1888. The town was supposed to be called McGlathery; no one could spell it nor pronounce it.

The first school was built in 1894 in the lower floor of the Masonic Lodge. It was where the Mercer Baptist Church now stands. Early teachers were J. J. Pennington, Professor Holt and Professor G. R. Winds. About 1908, two rooms were added, one upstairs and one downstairs and by then the faculty included professor Winds, Miss Sally Fletcher, Miss Kate Sharp and Miss Mary Reid.

A new brick school was built in 1912, it was built on the top of the hill on what is now Midget Street. Science and home economics were added. The first class to graduate from the new building included Celia Glenn, Alava Turner, Elizabeth Reid, Lela Mai Teer and Fred Siler. When the Armistice was signed, November 11, 1918, Professor Winds turned out the school and led the student body in a parade down town.

Mr. Fenner Lee Pope operated a livery business adjacent to Mercer He boarded at the Pennington Hotel, across the street from that train station. He married Mary Frank Ragland on September 6, 1911. She was the daughter of Dr. Walter Ragland who had the first drug store in Mercer. Annie Sue, their daughter was born June 3, 1913. After their marriage they continued living at the hotel until they purchased the McGlathery house from Will S. Nucholls. Fenner and Mary Frank had another daughter, Madeline Elizabeth born December 21, 1917.

Martha Elizabeth Mercer McGlathery (Mattie,) died October 4th, 1896. She is buried at Maple Springs. Franklin sold his interest in Mercer/McGlathery Store to his brother-in-law Col T. E. Mercer. He sold the house to Nucholls and moved his family to Paducah, Ky. He remarried Ella Cartwright in 1900. He became a very wealthy man involved in real estate in Kentucky.

On April 30, 1857, some 27 years before Mercer became a town, Mr. Miles C. Hayes for "love and affection," for the Methodist Episcopal Church South conveyed to M B. Sherman, David Meriwether, T.M. Sipes, J. B. Campbell, H. Barrier, trustees 2 acres in Civil District 4, Madison County, as long as the land was used for religious purposes of this church. "Also I am to have a family burying ground on said.....of land and that it is not to be a public burying ground.

Miles C. Hayes died in 1868 leaving no widow, but seven children. His land had to be sold because one son was deceased and it was deemed unfair to his minor children, who lived out of state to divide the land. November 12, 1870 the Hays land was sold at the court house. His children bought some of the land. James Hays bought 103 acres in lot #1, the Church and graveyard is

The Masonic Lodge upstairs over the Denmark Presbyterian Church. The Denmark Lodge #154 was first chartered in 1828. Early Worshipful Masters were: T. D. Tarver, J. R. Alston, Lewis T. Williamon, T. M Meriwether, W. A. Morgan, W. M. Henry, Thomas Bond, H. P. Hudson, W. D. Fletcher, W. D Utley, A.R. Reid and L.B. Campbell. This area was also use as a prison after the Battel of Briton Lane.

mentioned in every deed since 1857. It has now been deeded to Mercer Baptist Church.

There are 38 Civil War soldiers buried in a trench here. Mr. Hays and a black slave moved them from a spot down the road where they were ambushed. It took four wagons to move them. There is a marker by the trench. The story is that Fielding Hurst killed them and threw the bodies in "the murder hole." Mr. Hays recovered them from this ditch.

Another very interesting resident of Mercer was Mrs. Classie Robertson, midwife. She says, "I don't know how many babies I delivered but the doctor said I hold the record. Mrs. Classie's house caught on fire and when they rescued the mattress from the burning house they found it was filled with money. She is buried in the Ebenezer Cemetery. Every day, "Aunt" Classie Robertson would come down town Mercer to the store to "set a spell," and visit, maybe have a soft drink. At this time she was 91.

At one time Mercer had four doctors, a drugstore, a bank, a hotel, the NC & St. L Railroad Station and several other general stores, one Pennington's sold coffins.

Billy King

The Southern Methodist Episcopal Cemetery in Denmark, Tennessee

221

Thomas E. Mercer

Thomas E. was an enterprising merchant originally from Toone, Tennessee and a member of the firm of Mercer & McGlathery. He was a native of Madison County born February 5, 1844, the fourth of eight children, son of Thomas B. And Catherine (Crisum.) His parents were married in Madison County about 1830 and then moved to Hardeman County in 1843. His father was born in Currituck County N. C. December 1816. He was a farmer and Democrat and a member of the Missionary Baptist Church. His mother was a member of the same church; she was born in Middle Tennessee in 1818. When Thomas was seventeen he enlisted in Company B, Thirty-third Tennessee Regiment Infantry in Chatham's Division and participated in battles of Shiloh, Perryville, KY, Murfreesboro and Chickamauga. He was wounded with severe wounds at Chickamauga. After he recovered, he returned to service, but was official placed on the retired list at Greensboro, Ga. In July 1864 he returned to Tennessee and re-entered school, and after completing his education, he engaged as a clerk in different mercantile houses for five years. In 1869 he formed a partnership with a brother, W. A. Mercer, and James Little and opened a grocery store in Toone. In 1883 the brother sold his interest to F. M. McGlathery. September 6, 1870 Thomas married Miss Lizzie Cartwright. When his sister died, Mattie Mercer, Franklin married Lizzie Cartwright's sister.

* * *

Along Rural By-Paths (The Sport of Kings)

By FONVILLE NEVILLE

The sport of kings was not infrequently on the calendar of events in the early days of old Denmark. There were two stretches of road, level and straight, just beyond the town's limits¯Johnson's flat on the Brownsville road and the Sand flat on the Center Point road. On these the landed gentry tried out their trotters and pacers not only against time but against each other. Not far from Estanaula Ferry was a mile circular track where a county-wide gathering of the sporting fraternity occurred twice a year. Good blood was there. One of the best of the racers¯Grey Eagle¯was owned by James Alston of Denmark.

He won a sweepstakes' race at Estanaula and was entered against some of the best horses in the south at

Jackson when Mr. Alston got religion.

It was at the first camp meeting ever held in the Big Hatchie country. Strangely enough Mr. Alston himself was one of the chief powers behind its initiation. It proved also his regeneration and despite the fact that quite a bit of money had been wagered on the race by his friends he withdrew Grey Eagle and sold him to the highest bidder.

However Denmark had not seen its last racer, nor its last race. Many years down from Grey Eagle's day a race took place in which two of the town's most prominent ladies took part-a leading part, and which today lingers more cherished in the memories of old chronicles than any race won by the famous Grey Eagle.

Seen infrequently now are the caravans which in the old days wended their way along the roads to pitch their camps near the small villages and communities. Gypsies, they, were called but horse trading was their game.

Nothing was barred, and in those times the matching of wits in horse flesh afforded no end of excitement.

Trading for excitement and trading for profit are two different things. It usually ended in the townsfolk getting the excitement and the gypsies the profit.

Quite so with one gentleman whose trading instinct exceeded his judgment. He spent one entire afternoon dickering, returning home about nightfall with the fruits.

"This is a race horse," he proudly announced to his wife.

"Shades of Don Quixote!" gasped his wife. "Rocinante in the flesh!"

"Who?" asked the not so literary husband.

For answer, a wave of the hand that consigned himself and the steed into the limbo of the hopeless. He turned and surveyed his latest transition of horseflesh.

Now that his blood had cooled, he saw clearly what had been foisted off on him, and the result of his conclusions was an unwitting agreement with his wife. Ignorant of that steed of fiction which galloped through the pages of a knighthood satire to fame and immorality, he was forced to concede that it would be a long day's journey to find the equal of what he had acquired. Lest the buzzards would have long picked clean. He sighed, "well, dad-gum it! He's a race horse."

Under careful grooming the race horse lost some of its amazing angles, although it remained best described than seen. The seclusion of a stall when acclaimed "my race horse," often saved the owner's reputation. However the day came when it was allowed the run of distant pasture. And as all things come to the hour, so came the need of Rocinante which the wife had in biting jest labeled the animal.

It was a churchly emergency. Nothing less would have placed the lady upon the dependence of such a creature, lacking the pulchritude of any of its kind, resembling rather a carpenter's saw buck ambling across the fields. But it was the fourth Sunday at Ebenezer and homecoming day. Every vehicle was filled; every conveyance possibility exhausted, so perforce it Rocinante or walk.

Miss Jude, as we'll call the lady, not her name and all but one to convey to you the rigorousness of her temperament and the cast iron severity of her countenance. Her companion, bold enough to attempt the trip and yet add zest to it, we'll name Miss Julie, hoping that her name will imply her abundance of figure and kittenish ways.

"Tell Miss Julie," said Miss Jude to the Negro boy, "to be sure and put on her duster, as I am certain we'll have to take every one's dust and she'll know what that means. The roads as dry as they… are just dust beds.

There was not room on either side of the road to pass. To swing the slow moving beast to the side in the time was out of the question, although with whip and voice the driver was doing his utmost.

What he saw he doubted existed. A creature which in few details resembled a horse tearing down on him at express train speed, head stretched to the limit of a eves neck, tail without scant herbage streaming out behind in the faces of two figures whose sex he was at a difficulty to distinguish.

The crash seemed inevitable. He took refuge in a ditch. Miss Julie opened her mouth to indulge in one last dying shriek only to have it filled with what hairs remained on Rocinante's tail. Miss Jude dropped the reins and covered her face with her hands.

The slackened reins meant but one thing to Rocinante⁻the race was finished. The fire went out of her and in ten feet she was standing stone still. In three seconds she was sound asleep.

* * *

Along Rural By-Paths (Wet)

By FONVILLE NEVILLE

One of Denmark's prominent citizens voted "wet" in the recent election. But upon arriving home went drier than the sands of the Saharan under the barrage of glances leveled at him by his wife. His switch of sentiment he explained⁻ "The Dog on ticket was so complicated that I made a mistake."

All of which brings back the time when Denmark went dry and another man made a mistake. It was fifty years ago and the man was Lemy Wallick.

"I'm wet," stated Lemy, a day now years gone, placing his glass on the bar with ringing emphasis, "And I don't care who knows it. Them's my sentiments and that's how I'm going to vote tomorrow." His five feet of height and hundred pounds of weight bristled aggressively.

"One thing certain," observed Dad French, servitor of the thirsty, "How a fellow votes will sure be known."

"Which is to be the wet side?" asked Lemy.

"This one. The dry's will line up on the other."

"And I'm going to stand right in front of your door,

Dad," stated Lemy with the air of one whose confers both an honor and a favor.

"Well," said Dad slowly, in his mind's eye came a picture of Lemy's three hundred pound wife. "I'm glad your sentiments are like that, but if it is just the same to you I'd rather you'd stand a little to one side. My doors are glass and glass doors cost money these days."

Dad hadn't the only saloon in town. There were four others. Besides almost every store‾dry goods and grocery–sold whiskey. Some had basements; some dispensed it from barrels in the rear. Dad's place was the best. Mahogany bar, brass rail, mirrors; eating place in the rear. A basement whence hurried and secretive exit could be accomplished in the interest of Home Sweet Home. Also Dad was quick on alibis and could furnish them with impressiveness of a Chinaman.

A wave of reform had swept the town. Whiskey had to go with its accompanying evils. To avoid the expense usually entailed it was proposed and accepted that one side of the street be designated as dry; the other wet. A man voted his sentiments by going to the side of his choice.

It was two days before the election that Lemy laid

down his ultimatum, which ultimatum he wound about him more tenaciously than the serpents wound about Leocoon as that day increased, so great was his indignation.

The next day was but a repetition of the other, only that to indignation he added foolhardiness by stating that he'd vote drinking a toast to the cause he espoused so ardently.

Mike Burton who had loaned Lemy some money stopped him.

"Look here, Lemy," he drawled. "Ain't you going about this thing a bit too strong. Your wife's going to be home that day?"

Full of Dutch courage Lemy snapped. "Yes. But what of that?" No woman votes me."

"Amen," said Mr. Burton. "Suppose then you rustle up that money you owe me in case something should happen."

Election Day dawned. The voting was to start at nine o'clock. Only actual residents of the town would be allowed to vote. But from the surrounding country as early as daylight people began to pour in. Wet and dry, their influence would be exerted.

The Merriwether's had a saloon (or Doggery as it was called,) across the street from the Denmark Presbyterian Church. Tom Reid was home on leave and going to the doggery, not realizing that the 30th Illinois was marching into town behind him; when he realized it, he crawled under the Church to hide. The problem was, they camped on the lawn of the Church and he could not get out. When it got dark, he crawled out under the Church bell and began tolling the bell, causing all the horses to break loose. In all the commotion he got over to the doggery. The troops would come into Denmark often from the camps at Estonallie and would use the Church grounds as a camping site. The night before the Battle of Britton Land, the 30th was camped there and the night after the battle, the Southern Troops were camped there. They had put their prisoners upstairs in the Masonic Lodge.

* * *

Commercial Appeal

April 30, 1872

The Mass meeting in Denmark, Tennessee on behalf of a narrow gauge railroad was attended by a large and enthusiastic crowd yesterday. Col. A. W. Campbell and Col. John D. Logan made speeches which were heartily applauded. There is every evidence that the subscriptions necessary to make this railroad a reality will be forthcoming very soon.

* * *

Denmark Meetings Lined Before Railroads Passed By and Settlement Pined

By FONVILLE NEVILLE

Denmark, the village to the southwest of Jackson, was once a prosperous, happy and hopeful town, but has suffered disastrous fires, and the railroads missed it. Many prominent families of Denmark have sought prosperity in Jackson and other places.

In 1928, John Johnston, then in his 87th year and successful attorney in Memphis wrote a letter to Fonville

Neville of Denmark in response to a request that Mr. Neville made him. John Johnston's recollections of his early days in Denmark was one of the most interesting documents that has been located concerning this little town.

According to the account of those days, an old Indian trail came down from Kentucky to Denmark. The trace crossed the Hatchie River at Estanaula, thence to Fayette Corner near the present town of Whiteville, and then on to the Chickasaw Bluffs. There was plenty of evidence that there was once an Indian settlement at Denmark, for year's later flint, arrowheads, other stone implements, and bits of broken pottery could be found near the Indian mounds on the Estanaula Road.

Some of the earliest settlers in his section of the county during the decade from 1820 to 1830 came from North Carolina, South Carolina and Virginia, among them the Meriwethers. Alstons, Bryans and Johnstons. About this time, and the years immediately following, came the Neely's, Harts, Alexander's, Tyron's, McBride's, Reid's, Rice's, Bonds, Williamsons, Murchison's, Moors, McMillians, Utley's. Robertson's and many others. The first store was located on Big Black Creek by the Harbert's who later moved the store to Denmark. By 1840 there were seven or eight dry goods retail stores in the town, which could also boast of John Wray's grocery store, "doggery" or whiskey shop, and the old Meriwether hotel.

The old stage road passed through Denmark on to Estanaula and from thence to Memphis. Estanaula itself was a place of interest, for it was an important shipping point in this section. Sometimes the farmers hauled their cotton by wagon to Memphis. But more often they brought it to Estanaula, stored it in warehouse kept by Mr. Bumpus and, shipped it to Memphis by boat. They brought back provisions by boat and stayed at a hotel kept by Archie McBride while they were transacting business.

The people of this community had two principle interests beyond making a living, the church and as John Johnston remembered it the old female academy located on the slope of the hill a little east of where the Methodist church once stood. Here the Misses Emina and Talinda Senesman instructed the young ladies of the adjoining counties. Many students from the adjoining counties came here to attend the female academy under the direction of A. M. Lewis, or the male academy under W. Slack, Tom Norvel and Mr. Howard.

The Presbyterian Church was the center of interest

in the midst of a young throng of fine people. The Hopewell Church organized by John Wharton, David Weir and Robert Johnston was combined on February 3, 1833 with the few Presbyterians at Denmark, the organization becoming known as the "Presbyterian Church in Denmark." All denominations attended the Sunday school while preaching on the Sabbath and Wednesday nights was well attended Rev. James Gillespie, the minister for 25 years, was faithful, reverent and dignified. The old church built about 1846, stands on the south side of the Main Street just where the Jackson road runs into the ravine leading down into Sandy Bottom.

This was a normal community, so there was the ever-present need to guide the conduct of some of the people; but there was a strong moral influence of the church, especially the old Presbyterian. There were no dances, no card parties, no divorces, and there were many seasons of great revivals, when all were profoundly impressed with Divine and Holy things and the power of the world to come. The great revival of a century ago was under the preaching of Daniel Baker. On a hill near the old Phillip Alston home on the Jackson-Denmark road stood a large shed, resting upon upright pillars hewn out of solid timbers, looking something like an old fashioned gin house. Later Philip Alston boarded this up for a barn, but it was built as a meeting place for the famous Daniel Baker revivals.

The people came in throngs to this revival in 1847; they brought volumes of the preacher's published sermons with them. They were astonished that he delivered "offhand" these powerful sermons that were designed to create "mental excitement strong enough to produce great anxiety, strong enough to keep the eyes wakeful through the night and occasionally tears, and sometimes sobbing in the prayer meetings and the house of God." But the words of God spoken by this powerful preacher were so inspired that the campers soon forgot themselves and laid aside the written sermons, completely captivated by the dire and eloquence of the speaker which could not possibly be put on paper.

When the era of railroad building came, the people of Denmark community began to move away for the Mobile and Ohio Railroad which passed through Jackson and missed Denmark. The real death knell was sounded when the two railroads proposed in the latter part the nineteenth century passed the village by. An old directory of 1872 tells of how enthusiastic the people were over these two roads–The Tennessee Midland and the Denmark, Brownsville and Durhamville. (There was a

Civil War Battle at Durhamville, Fayette County, TN.) The citizens subscribed $25,000 to the latter road, but this road never got beyond a few hundred feet of embankment built through a field west of Brownsville. The failure of this road probably accounted for the refusal of the citizens to accede to a demand made by the Tennessee Midland Railroad for $3,000. Upon the mistaken premise that the road would be forced to come through anyway, because of Big Black Creek bottom they sat still and did nothing. Consequently the road was built a bit south. The village of Mercer grew overnight and Denmark entered upon a steady decline.

Fate was seemingly working against the growth of Denmark. In 1860, seventeen stores burned; in 1867, a fire destroyed almost the entire business section. In 1903, three stores burned; twelve buildings including a cotton gin have burned since 1924.

Preached as Pals Stole
Denmark Church Aided in War
By FONVILLE NEVILLE

The HISTORIC Presbyterian church of Denmark, Tenn., shown here with its present pastor, Rev. James F. Pharr, has been the scene of many stirring events during its more than 100 years of existence.

On a bleak December day in 1924, John Wharton and family of five, with Robert Johnson and family of seven, gathered in a log hut on the banks of a small stream called Club Creek, four miles north of Denmark, where, assisted by Rev. David Weir, they organized a Presbyterian Church, calling it Hopewell. This church became the parent of the present Denmark Presbyterian Church, whose congregation worships in the old frame building, shown in the picture, which was erected on 1854.

The records do not show how long Rev. Weir served. He was succeeded by Rev. Samuel Hodge, who not only served as pastor of this church but went thru the sparsely settled country preaching in homes and school houses.

Under the leadership of Rev. A. A. Campbell, of Virginia, this congregation was merged with a small

The L. M. Wilson Gin crew at Leighton, Tennessee, left to right back row, Robert Taylor Curlin, Jamie Boggs, Wilson Thomas, Bernie Pentecost and Lewis Bond, kenneling, Willie "wild cat' Kenny, and State Bond. The first gin at Leighton was Curlin and Curlin. The old L. M. Wilson Gin is still standing at the corner of U.S.Hwy. 138 and Denmark/Woodland Road in Madison County, TN. .

congregation at Denmark on February 23, 1833. On April 5 of that year, the church was admitted into the Memphis Presbytery. At that time, it was worshipping in a small log house about 100 yards east of the present building. The log house had been raised in six days and was christened "Jonah's Gourd."

Heard Bandit Preach

It was under the pastorate of Rev. Alexander McNutt that the first camp meeting was introduced into the Denmark community, services being held at Black Spring, a mile south of the village. In addition to serving as pastor, Rev. McNutt taught school in a log house at Jackson, Tenn., where the present Union railroad station stands.

If the old building could speak, it could tell many interesting things that have happened on its premises. John A. Murrell, a noted bandit of his day, once occupied its pulpit and repenting of all his sins, but while he was repenting, his gang was outside stealing the horses of the congregation.

Bell is Fire Alarm

Its huge bell can be heard seven miles away and has served as a fire alarm for many years. Since 1840, some member of the Hart family has been connected with the board of elders. James Hart being the first elected to that position on September 28th, that year.

That day is also noted in the church's history for one other interesting record. Jim Hart and Thomas Alston were elected at that time as choristers. When they began their work, an argument arose about the use of a musical instrument in the church services. For a time this quarrel threatened the life of the church. Those wanting the organ yielded and it was not until 42 years later that the Denmark Presbyterian Church began to use a musical instrument at its service. Miss Mattie Love was the first organist and later became the wife of Rev. C. C. Weaver, who was afterwards pastor of the First Presbyterian Church of Oklahoma City.

The church has had 22 different pastors. While the community is small, at one time it membership was 170. Now there are about 60 with only 40 considered active members. The present board of elders is W. T. West, J. E. Reid, W. L. Taylor, C. V. Hart and J. N. Hart.

ALONG RURAL BY-PATHS (Romances)
By FONVILLE NEVILLE

Among the many romances of old Denmark whose memory like license rises to sweeten the dissolution old age has wrought is the one of John Wildstadt and Mary Waddell. Occurring in the early '50s even the legend is almost forgotten. Mary Waddell under another name sleeps in the shadows of the family tomb upon a hill. On another hill beneath sighing cedars is the dust of John Wildstadt in an unmarked grave. Once it bore a simple stone on which was engraved briefly "John Wildstadt, Peddler."

No fame or eulogy is here supplied, but in that simple, brief inscription lies the story.

Industry, wealth and culture were the potentates wielding scepters in the village when John Wildstadt came down the Estanaula road with an oil skin pack on his back.

Fair and rich lay the fields across the wealth of which gleamed the white colonnades of manorial houses. To these came John Wildstadt, crowned with a winning

William (Bill) Harbert and Mary Wadell Harbert

William and his brother John opened one of the first trading post on the banks of Big Black Creek in conjunction with the Chickasaw Indians. When West Tennessee became a part of Tennessee (Treaty 1818) and the Post office of Denmark was opened (1820) they moved the trading post to Denmark. There are many stories of Bill. He and John became some of the wealthiest people in West Tennessee. Bill married Mary when she was 17 and he was 30. Bill sold his land and interest in the store to his brother and he and his family moved to Texas, all 150 of his slaves went with him. He sent his brother Stephen ahead to buy land, they were cousins of David Crocket, their mother was a Crocket. We do not know where they are buried. The Wadell's are buried in Big Black Creek Baptist and two in Denmark Methodist. Mary may be in one of the Denmark Cemeteries, they married in the Old Denmark Presbyterian Church.

smile, and queer musical words which stood romance at his side.

There was something about him which opened all doors, mansion and cabin. Mid the mundane articles of his pack lay some little trinket of a far off land which glossed the rest with an air of mystery and glamor. Such prosaic things as shoe strings and hair pins took on unproportionate color and charm.

His coming and goings had been many before the day Mary Waddell came back from school. On that day with the familiarity of an old custom he dropped his pack between the white pillars and sank upon the steps.

"Ho, Mammy Caroline. I have a head rag here that'll make your eyes shine like a coachman's buttons. And a glass of cold milk gets it."

"Aside from head rags," said a silken voice from the door. "Have you any side combs?"

In the act of sinking down upon a step he straightened–caught himself at the edge of a transformation. "Pardon me, miss, you startled me. You were not here before when I came."

"No, I'm just back from school. I broke my comb

last night. It came from Vienna and I was grieving about it when Mammy Caroline said you'd be along today. And most likely would have one like it."

He undid his pack, produced a comb. Mary Waddell placed it in her hair. "Oh," she said. "I never thought a peddler carried such things so rare!"

"The queen wore one some months ago," he said. "I thought perhaps they'd become the fashion soon. I bought several."

"It looks much better on you than the queen," he added.

"You've been there? You've seen the queen?" she asked.

"City of sham and vanity," he muttered. Then to her- "I lived there once."

When he turned his face toward the road there was on it what had no right on the face of a peddler.

Whenever they say he looked across sunlit fields, he saw a colonial doorway framing a portrait whose sheen of raven hair, twin lakes of homeland blue and contour of form set a song in his heart that his lips were incapable of uttering.

Mary dreamed strange fantasies that night in the moonlight, the courtly grace which had suddenly cloaked the peddler at her greeting. The "something" behind his character when he spoke of old Vienna. But romance did not come riding in the guise of a peddler, no matter if his head was chiseled like a king's and his manners like a prince. "Shame on you, Mary Waddell!" she would cry, and straightway fall to dreaming again.

John Wildstadt came again and again. Much too often for the needs of commerce, a picture in his heart, the memory of a voice in his ear, turned his feet from under the weight of his hundred and fifty pound pack as if it were naught, flinging to whoever was in sight a jovial greeting couched in the language of his homeland. Even the austere dignity of the major bent to his infectious gaiety. And Mary would come to the door and he'd bring from his pack whole new baubles of fashion.

They'd sit in the soft light, he with back against a white pillar telling her of distant land, strange places, and cities old and famous. He talked as one who had shared rather than viewed their greatness.

"Did you peddle in all those places?" she asked.

"Yes-" he hesitated a moment, "yes-peddle," he said,

but the significance he put on the word could have any of a thousand meanings.

To Mary Waddell cloistered in her old southern home, he, with his tales of far places, his laughter and queer songs, his pack stripped from his back, was no peddler–how she hated the odium of that name¯but a knight errant, some far flung descendant of medieval days when knighthood took to the road in quest of romance and adventure in guises best suited to their purpose. It was only when he went swinging down the drive, bent beneath his pack, that the spell was broken. "Only a peddler¯peddler!" she'd whisper to herself to quiet the tumult of her heart.

Of this barrier John Waldstadt was aware, though it rose not often between them in their talks, and it did in sudden restraint on Mary's part, his eyes would sometimes show hurt of light with an inward amazement.

Never a word of love did he speak. But his eyes spoke for him, and everything in the girl sprang to meet their message.

He came that last time, his pack a thing apart, and stood before her smiling tenderly, eyes lighted with the promise of a wondrous surprise. There was a certain princely bearing his rough but clean clothes could not deny. "Mary," he cried, "I⁻"

She lifted a hand while the other crept to her bodice. How she had dreaded this moment. "I am the wife of Calvin Tarbert (Mr. Fonville substituted his real name, it was William Harbert). We were married a fortnight ago."

With a gesture he dropped the pack between them. "Was it that?" he asked.

She nodded dumbly.

His eyes grew dark⁻ then softened. "You love me!" he whispered.

His answer flashed unhidden across her face. White and trembling she sank back against a pillar.

"But a Waddell could not marry a peddler. I was not going to ask you to do that, dear. But I waited too long. I waited too long."

"What do you mean?" she cried.

He shook his head. "It would not matter now."

Mary married Bill Harbert and they built a house still standing in Denmark. They eventually moved to Texas. There are four Weddell graves in Big Black Creek

Baptist Cemetery with large slabs over them. There are two at Methodist, they died in New Orleans in 1909 and the bodies shipped back to Denmark. There is a little fence around these graves, the fence maker is still in existence in St. Louis.

* * *

Jackson Gazette, No. 28, Vol. VI., Jan 2, 1830

Married on Thursday evening, Mr. WM. Harbert of Denmark, to Miss Mary Waddle daughter of WM. Waddell, Esq. of this county. In this county, Doctor Samuel W. Vaughn of Denmark, to Miss Martha W. Turner.

John, William, Mary, Stephen's mother was Sarah (Sallie) Crockett Harbert, the aunt of David Crockett. Mary married T. B. Rice.

William (Bill) and Mary built their first house in 1831. It was sold to Bill's brother Dan, when Bill and Mary went to Texas. The house still stands in Denmark across the street from the Denmark Presbyterian Church. The Harbert's owned the largest merchantile establishment in the Big Hatchie country. The house is called Pear Grove, the front hall is 10 feet wide, with the back door at the other end. On each side of the hall are three very large rooms, the four corner ones having fireplaces. The ceilings are 13 feet high, the windows 10 feet with six over-six panes. The kitchen and eating area are under the house. It is said a engineer from Pennsylvania designed the house. It is known that a engineer from Pennsylvania designed the Reid House also and maybe the Denmark Presbyterian Church, Union Grove Presbyterian Church and Chestnut Presbyterian Church.

The House was eventually sold to the Hardee family and is often referred to as the Hardee house. Lemuel Hardee (1838-1916) was born October 18, 1838 in Johnston County, North Carolina to Magear (Major) John Hardee and Elizabeth Mewborn. Lemuel's mother died but we do not know the date. On April 7, 1849 Lemuel's father died. Lemuel is mentioned several times in his fathers will. From the will, "Negroes Winifred and Sarah to be sold, debts paid and any money remaining put in interest until son Lemuel Hardee, a minor reaches 21 in Oct. 1859. All other interest to be equally devided among all children. Negroes Handy, Prince, Jacob and Richard to be hired out until son Lemuel is 21". Lemuel married Aphia Adaline Utley in North Carolina. They moved to West Tennessee around 1860. The country's

George Hardee   Lemuel Hardee   Lon Hardee

Civil War was in full swing and growing closer to home. Lemuel enlisted in the Confederacy on 8 Jul. 1863 in Denmark during a raid behind Federal lines.

An excerpt from the Civil War Questionnaire made by the 83 year old John Ambrose Reid indicated he remembered Lemuel as a member of his regiment....in this statement he mentions many of the men from Denmark who were serving. One is the son of the pastor of the Denmark Church, Pvt. John Gillispie, who was wounded and sent home where he died. Reid states that Lemuel was a member of Company C, 14 Tenn. Reg. Cavalry. He was paroled in Brownsville, Haywood County on 31 May, 1865 as a Prisoner of War. Lemuel is buried in the Denmark Presbyterian Cemetery, so is John Gillispie. *Jackie Utley*

* * *

DOOR THAT LED TO HAPPINESS

By FONVILLE NEVILLE

You come over a hill and there is the little cabin before you across the creek, atop another hill.

You cross the bridge, make a gentle curve, ascend the hill, swerve to your right and come upon the two-room cabin in the corner made by the road. You always had the feeling it was waiting for you.

It sits in a neatly kept yard, the ground dropping away in a gentle slope on all sides; the other boundaries are bushes and red soil of unfertile fields. It sits there despite its lack of splendor in a sort of regal contentment, as if apart from the rest of the scene, a world of itself.

And it is most of the world for the two colored people who live there, Uncle Ikle and Aunt Kenny.

Uncle Ike is always around, messing in his little garden or corn patch, be it Spring or Summer, a weather eye out for you.

If you stop at the mail box, he hurries forward with a faint, lopsided grin on his furrowed face; if you don't stop, he straightens his old back from whatever task he is doing and gives you an elaborate acknowledgement of your passing.

Aunt Kenny will be in the open door. She will ask, "How you getting' 'long dis fine mawning,' Mist' Mailman?"

"I'm all right, Aunt Kenny. How you makin' it?"

"I'm makin' hit fine." Her tone never changes-high.

"I'm makin' hit fine by the help o' de Lawd. You tek keer o' yourself. I don't know what I'd do efen I didn't hear you pass here ever day."

If you didn't stop you'd always look to see if she was standing in the door.

One day in each month Uncle Ikle wouldn't be around. You'd know he had gone to town to get supplies with the small monthly pension. Aunt Kenny would be in the door, and you couldn't pass.

Spring, dogwood would be blooming on every sky-lined hill, along the borders of the road and wood, in fence corners, lifting banners of white from the yet Winter shadowed bushes. The willows along the creek would be taking on a faint tint of green.

"Ain't you glad hit's Spring?" Aunt Kenny would say. "I know you are atter the Winter. I knows that Winter is yore moanin' time."

"You can see all the world from here, Aunt Kenny," you'd say. "Hill and bottom, and all dressing up with dogwood blossoms."

Her mouth would tighten a bit. "Hit sho' is a pretty sight," she'd reply. You'd feel sorry you had mentioned the dogwood.

Come Winter the little cabin would be shut tight; doors, windows barred against the cold, a citadel against the grayness all around.

Uncle Ike would be outside when you came along, getting in wood or doing some other chore. He shakes his head, grimaces and draws up his shoulders to express how bad it was. Sometimes he'd watch to see if the car would get through the mud hole that invariably yawned every winter more than axle deep at the foot of the hill. You didn't see much of Aunt Kenny, and you hoped she had heard you pass.

Now and then you'd stop with a letter from the "baby boy" out in California. As soon as you stopped, out of the house would pop Uncle Ike. That's how they listened.

If the wind was not too bitter, Aunt Kenny would come to the door Uncle Ike had left open. With her face lifted toward the sky, she would ask how you was getting along and how you was making it over muddy roads.

"Hit's yore moanin' time. I hears you go by ever' day an' I prays de good Lawd that nothin' won't happen to you. I'se got to hear you go by kase I knows by that there's another world out there somewhere I'se never seen."

Just the inside of the two-room cabin, the small yard, the road that ran by, the passing of the mailman was her world.

They seemed perfectly happy. Except…

There was one thing above all other things Aunt Kenny wanted. It was neither food nor drink nor clothes. She wanted a glass door.

It was an incongruous desire in the face of the many things she needed, useful and necessary, for comfort and health. Uncle Ike took a philosophical view. "Uf course she cain't eat hit ner wear hit," he thinks lak that sometimes, you know."

So the days went by until the morning you drive up the hill and drew abreast of the little cabin, something striking you as strange. Then you saw it, the glass door!

There it was hung in all its glory, shinning in the rays of the sun! An altar. A benediction.

Uncle Ike came out grinning, shaking his head. Aunt Kenny appeared, a hand resting in reverent gesture against the glass.

The occasion demanded it. You got out of the car and went to admire this odd fulfillment of a dream and hope. "You're happy now, I know, Aunt Kenny," you said.

* * *

SOUND OF GUNFIRE DISRUPTS QUIET OF DENMARK'S SUNDAY

(This is the first of a series on the Battle of Britton's Lane as prepared by Denmark's veteran historian.)

By FONVILLE NEVILLE

It lay peacefully under the warm morning sun of the new born month of September 1862, bordered on one side by a dyke of grey weathered chestnut rails, and on the other by a lip of earth and a skirt of wood-this strip of brown, dusty earth named Britton's Lane.

Its dust had risen from feet and wheels to settle a grey film on golden rod, iron weed and sumac which rose in clusters in the elbows of the wayward fence and strangled along the borders of its confines; on the rag weed that grew scantily from the lip of earth.

Trumpet vine ran its length along the lichen covered rails, weaved its scarlet blossoms between them to splotch their aged and weathered sides as it were with drops of blood.

Butterflies as if having drawn their color from the rods of gold they flew and floated and drifted in the bright sunlight above on Britton Lane. Black winged ones, others with greater gold and crimson and black plumage, seemingly borne on the soundless air without effort, rose and dipped above weed and flower, swept away to return again to lace the sunshine with varied brilliance.

A vagrant wind in a joyous mood dipped into its dust, raised it, danced with it an instant, then leaped the grey featured fiancé and whirled through the corn from which the leaves had been stripped with the gay bandon of a wanton child.

Summer's lingering breath laved all. A cloudless sky lay above. A solitary crow flew above it. From the skirt of wood a squirrel barked, in the branches flashed the blue crested wings of an errant jay.

In golden maturity the corn stood. Stripped of its fodder, it seemed stripped of companionship, it stood alone. At its roots twisted and twining upward about the columned grain morning glories lifted and thrust out cup shaped blossoms of blue. It seemed the earth bound and took up their hue to spread it like a mist with which to comfort the ground.

No presentment in the breath of the idle wind that wandered among the tasseled corn, stirring their bronze heads with such grace as to float them like banners.

No precluding whisper is the solemn silence which seemed to pay homage to the day man has chosen to worship his Maker, and yet which brought out of the distance the sound of church bells. There with brooding silence in a deflection of peace on earth that was soon to be no peace on earth; that has no desperation of itself but was all gave for the feet of men and hopes and down which come would walk to fame.

As the sun climbed high, the distant air began to mummer. Not with the voice of the future, nor did the dust that began to rise above the trees to some sudden gust of wind.

Then the silence became continuous as of the prelude that foretells a storm. The sound of marching men, the dull rumble of wheeled guns, the beautiful hooves of horses, drove away the butterflies.

The strip of dusty earth on which men in grey and white would clash, for which one would contend, seemed more than dust.

And one could well ask if death itself had not sent the shadow there, for in its not men were to die ushered to local history that which in time would make for immortality, Britton's Lane!

Thirteen-year-old Caledia Wilson, accompanied by her father, W. D. Wilson, were on their way to Sunday School that September morning of the first, 1862. As they joined others at the corner of the Meriweather Tavern that sat in the intersection of the Medon and Jackson road and took the two plank sidewalk to the Presbyterian Church, its bell was ringing.

It was 10 o'clock. Suddenly rising above the clanging of the bell, the chatter of voices, came a sullen sound out of the south like a clap of thunder.

It caused everybody to look up in surprise for there was not a cloud in the sky.

As they wondered, there came another sullen "Boom" then a minor sound like a pack of firecrackers set off. And as all stopped to listen, the sound rose and fell, the cannon spoke in intervals.

Strange interludes for this day of peace, strange intermingling of men's fury with his tokens of worship, for the church bells rang on…

There were three active churches in Denmark in 1862; they remained many years after–Baptist, Methodist, and Presbyterian. They ran together every Sunday morning. All had service every Sabbath.

To try to link up present day Denmark with those days is difficult indeed.

The Baptist and Methodist churches had belfries. Probably on account of the weight of the Presbyterian bell¯could have been because the building was two story¯it was hung outside on a frame of oak timbers.

Early that morning the 20th and 30th Illinois Infantry, commanded respectively by Capt. Fishbec and Maj. Shedd, under the general command of Col. Elias Dennis had broken camp made the night before in a grove of mulberry trees back of the church between the church and Charley Henry's dwelling, formed columns in what was known then as Back Street, then to the Medon road out by the McBride place.

In the van was Gumbert's Artillery of two small cannon, Battery B of the 2nd Illinois Artillery, thanks to

Harbert Alexander's article of Armstrong's West Tenn. Raid.

There is some confession about the two companies of Calvary, 4th Ohio, commanded by Capt. Foster.

Around 3 o'clock of the afternoon of Saturday Aug. 31, a troop of cavalry on the Center Point road, now the Huntersville road, that led north out of Denmark drew Nancy and James Reid out on the porch of their home, one mike north, erected in 1851, to watch the cavalry pass.

It set back from the road on a slight hill perhaps 200 yards and has Civil War history of its own, two sons in service. Besides that Col. Faulkner of a Kentucky regiment made it his headquarters while in this section. There he was surprised and almost captured.

The western side of the hill which the house faced once was shaded with a magnificent grove of oak trees.

Thomas Reid, brother of James, had built his house a mile farther down the road and surrounded it with cedars.

The 30th Illinois was coming down the road going to the Denmark Church grounds, this was a favorite camping site of the 30th. It was a sight to see, all dressed in their blues, with the canons and horses. At time it meant trouble for the Reid's, the troop would pillage the smoke houses and chicken houses for food. Mrs. Reid would hide her hams up over the front porch so they would not find them.

Mrs. Reid would raise pullets (frying size chickens,) to give to the northern army to keep them from stealing her hog meat. She would hide the hams over the front porch. Even today the grease still drops through the ceiling. We think the builder of this house was the same man who built the Denmark Presbyterian Church.

He was from Philadelphia and the time frame matches the buildings.

* * *

FIFTY YEARS TOGETHER

By FONVILLE NEVILLE

The first I knew I possessed strange powers was when I was little boy about ten years old. I had caught a bird in a trap and was bringing it to the house. Sitting under a tree to play with it, knowing mother would make me turn it loose. I fondled it, blowing on it with my breath. And the first thing I knew the bird was dead.

With the certain knowledge of the licking I would get, I was pretty worried and wondered what had caused it to die. I knew that I had now hit it or hurt it in getting it out of the trap. I puzzled about it for several days; and then boy-like the next bird I trapped I went through the same shenanigans‾rubbing it with my hands and blowing my breath on it and as before this bird toppled over dead.

Mr. Heidleberg, a long distant descendent of the Heidlebergs who in Germany found Heidleberg town, paused and eyed me closely.

We were gathered‾John Reynolds, Lee Byrum, Van Heidleberg and grandson‾in front of his home, the old Byrum place, celebrating the 50th anniversary of his wedding.

From the rear of the house came a grinding, not without a certain pleasant motif which suggested ice cream in the making. Footsteps clattered within and gay voices rang out as the children, grand and great, made ready for the anniversary feast.

From where we sat we could look across the fields of cotton and corn‾a flat, level and old land, brooding in a quietude which seemed to hold the spirit of all the years gone by. In distant vistas holding weather beaten and dull hued farm houses, visions seemed to rise from the old earth to people it again with the figure of those of whom we talked.

To the land yet clung the names and traditions of those who had hewed it from the wilderness; and there hung about the old buildings the rutted red earth, a mystical symbolism of those lives and of those times. The heritage of the land¯the fragrance of a long lost romance, the glory of a past era and the blight of tragedy the ghost hopes came as a wind from the old scenes to haunt us with memories. The oldest of us looked across the fields with dreaming eyes as if he were seeing the years rise up beyond the hills and beckon to him with visions.

Fifty years! What was fifty years to the old, old fields and hills? What one hundred? Or one thousand? What did Time and Life mean to these insensate watchers brooding through the centuries looking unmoved up generations of human drama…great themes, of love, joy, hope, despair, sorrow and pain made geniuses of poor actors, then swept them from the boards to be seen no more.

Now another play was drawing to a close. Fifty years it had run. Its leading man and lady had played every role in the farcical drama and now face to face with the last–the greatest scene of all, they hoped to take the last curtain call as they had begun the play‾ together.

Of course this was the day of days, and from this peak the hills and valleys of those 50 years looked neither so deep nor high. Mr. Heidleberg took them and the faithful companionship all for granted,

Of course he was proud. He was thankful. Proud that he had built their home with his hands; lived there forty years, and made a decent and honest living, earning the enmity of no man. Thankful he had been blessed with a mate who had never faltered nor complained; thankful that he had lived to be 74 and would leave no children to perpetuate his name.

Yes, these things were all right, but-

I got to fooling with a little grass snake one day like boys will do, thinking about the little bird. I made passes with my hands, then leaned over it and blew my breath on it.

Just pranking, mind you, with not an idea of what I was trying to do. But bless your soul, and I know you'll think I'm lying, the first thing I knew, and the snake had turned its white belly to the sun and died! Died just like those two birds had!

Right then and there I figured I had something queer wrong with me–that I was different from other folks. I went around killing snakes without end.

"A Saint Patrick," I murmured.

Mr. Heidleberg bowed. There must have been some French somewhere in his Germanic ancestry. Then his green little eyes looked at me dubiously.

"He killed snakes, too," I explained it. "He was gifted."

Mr. Heidleberg smiled. "Nobody can explain it. I can't. Some say I'm full of magnetism." He chuckled. "You knew Ben Ellison One day me and him and Mattie, his wife, were in the field. They were hoeing cotton. I was plowing. Suddenly I turned up a spreading adder. He was about three feet long. I called Ben to come over and watch me kill it.

Some folks didn't believe I could kill snakes like I did.

Ben came over, Mattie behind. The snake was wiggling off and I got in front of it and waved my hand over it, then bent down right quick and blew on it.

The snake stopped–seemed to draw up, then slowly

rolled over on its back all doubled up as if it had the colic.

Ben and Mattie stood there bug-eyed with wonder. Mattie said I had conjured it.

I told Ben I'd give him five dollars if when we came back the next morning the snake was gone if he'd give me something if it was still there. Ben said he had nothing to give sorter like he was afraid to get mixed up with me. The snake was there the next morning though the buzzards had eaten half of him, and I said to Ben if he would know exactly how the snake felt when I blew on it. Ben backed away from me like I was a ghost and Mattie got something out of her pocket and made a mark all around him.

John Reynolds, son-in-law, stretched out both of his hands, backs up. Not a blemish on them. "They used to be covered with warts," he said. "And he took 'em off."

Far and wide Uncle Andy was known for this almost seemingly miraculous power. Familiar with many of the superstitions connected with the practice, I asked if it was done by some secret formula or tie or by the magnetism he possessed.

I can't tell you how I do it. It's just something in

me. I rub the wart sometimes. Sometimes I just blow on it. But they go away. Fellow in Jackson had a thing on his upper eye-lid 'bout an inch long. It bothered him a lot and I asked him why he didn't have it taken off.

"He'd had it cut off but it always came back. Nothing would help it. Do you believe in conjure or hoodoo?" I asked him.

He looked at me funny-like, "I'd believe in anything that y'll take this thing off," he said.

I asked him then to let me blow my breath on it. He did and I blew on it three times. Two weeks later I went back and the thing gone. He offered to pay me but I wouldn't take his money.

"You don't have to wait for the moon to get right?" I asked.

"Moon?" Mr. Heidleberg looked at me as if I had suddenly gone foolish. "The moon's got nothing to do with it," he said indignantly.

I've a close friend who is a wart doctor. But his is done by a certain formula and with attending rites. The moon has to be right and he didn't come by it naturally. An old Negro so gifted passed it on to him when he died.

Anyone who tells the secret has his powers taken from him, so the old Negro waited until he was at death's door before he gave it up. But nothing like this with Uncle Andy. He is a natural.

Medical science denies such things. "Pshaw!" it says. "Ridiculous!" But nevertheless these things are irrefutable. It is the nearest approach to supernatural powers I've ever observed in a human being. To have a huge crescent on your hand gently massaged by the "doctor." Maybe he'll ask you not to watch him. Then put your hand behind you. Anyway in a few days after you've forgotten all about the affair you suddenly become aware that the wart is gone.

"There are more things under Heaven than are dreamed of in your philosophy, Horatio!"

Lee Byrum spoke up. "Only three people living today who were at Andy's wedding – me, Jim and Neely Miller."

"Out of that entire house full of people," put in Mr. Heidleberg. "It liked to have scared me to death when Squire Rufus Newsom who married us told me to salute the bride, fifty years ago," he murmured, "but it don't seem so long when you look back."

Watching the two with fifty years of married life behind them and but a few more ahead I wondered what they now thought of life. I could imagine them coming up through the years. At first eager, fresh and full of hopes and dreams. Then as illusions faded and hopes grew faint and dreams more difficult to dream, their steps slowed, their enthusiasm began to wane. Then the struggle for a star dropped to a struggle for a living, interest drew in, fastened upon each other. Then as the children left them alone and life a thing to be live instead of enjoyed they found in each other the answer to their disappointments, and lost dreams.

As it should be after fifty years.

Mr. Heidleberg summed it up better "She didn't cost me but two dollars and Fifty cents and it was the best bargain I ever made."

* * *

WHEN PIGEON WAS SHOT TOP OF OLD MADISON COURTHOUSE

By FONVILLE NEVILLE

(September 10, 1958)

Editor's Note – Fennville Neville, the author of this article had from time to time contributed similar stories to THE JACKSON SUN. He is a resident of Denmark and locally well-known as a historian.

What folks do is the core of history. Charley Harris and I were looking up some portion of it when we ran across a picture of the old red brick court house, clock tower on top, taken in 1912, a scattering of autos and top buggies in front.

"Lord, you remember how we used to love to come to town in those days," said Charley. "Got to come only about three times a year. Wake up in the middle of the night and hear that old clock bonging? What a thrill was in the grinding of buggy tires on the gravel streets, the clip-on of the horse's feet; what a heavenly smell was the smell of coal smoke!"

Betts and Robertson was where the post office

stands. C. N. Harris, book store, James and Nelson, drugs, on Main Street. The Peoples Savings Bank on the corner. It was in front of James and Nelson that Little Jackson shot a pigeon off the top of the court house.

"Now hold on!"

The God's truth! He tried out a new gun he'd just bought from Gilbert Anderson. He had the biggest hardware store in the county where Black and White was. Little Jackson and two others, Friction and Cuffy, came to town for the day. Little Jackson to get a shotgun. Friction had business at the court house. Cuffy no doubt had a note due at the bank.

You know how it was in those days when country fellers got to town, eight or ten salons scattered around. King's Palace in full blast, too.

They had dinner at the Gem Café. Little Jackson couldn't eat all his. He called a waiter to bring him a paper sack.

You know how close little Jackson was, tighter than Cleotheses.

Cleotheses?

The fellow Dante wrote about who got in Heaven

on a dime and then wanted a rebate.

Little Jackson put his leavings in the paper sack to bring home to his dog, he said. But Friction and Cuffy knew who he was bringing it home for.

After dinner they went to Baum's Poolroom to shoot a game or two of pool. Cuffy had by this time got so he couldn't see so well, punching holes in the cloth. They were asked to leave.

"About time to go home and Little Jackson went and got his gun, a twelve gauge single barrel Stevens.

"A cautious man as to how he spent his money, wanting the most he could get for it, he debated quite a while over its merits, wishing he could try it out. Of course there was no place for this, so he finally bought it. Six dollars. Think of buying a new gun that cheap now.

"They started to the livery stable. Coming down Main Gene, after a certain brand of humor he possessed, began needling Little Jackson about the gun. Right in front of James and Nelson's."

"Why the doggone thing might not even shoot. Could be something wrong with the plunger or hammer, caused it to miss fire. You'd hate to line up a squirrel for dinner and the doggone thing snapped. Or maybe it's too full chocked for squirrels. Looks to me like the sight is crooked."

"He got Little Jackson worrying right."

"Tell you what," said Friction, "why don't you try it out before we go home. Then if anything's the matter you can get your money back."

"Wish I could."

Friction's eyes roved around. "See if it'll kill one of those pigeons on top of the court house."

"You remember how the pigeons need to congregate there hardly ever still, strutting about and cooing.

Little Jackson unwrapped the gun, loaded it, waited until one of the feathered congregation got still and let fly.

Course shooting a gun on Main Street was against the law and caused a lot of commotion.

By the time a policeman got there they were around the corner out of sight.

Little Jackson got the pigeon all right. But if he

hadn't, it wouldn't be the gun's fault. A fellow who could be persuaded to shoot a gun on Main Street was bound to have been bleary eyed.

In the early days of Jackson, there were several salons, one was called Court Alley Tap Room, and it was in an alley across from the old Court House. It had a long troth down the bottom of the bar, so you could just stand at the bar and relieve yourself and not have to go outside. Women were not allowed in some of the early bars. This one catered to lawyers who had been at the Court House. I am sure that some of the doggary's (salons) in Denmark had these troths.

* * *

People who have contributed to this work:

Mrs. Nevelle Stewart

Mr. Harbert Alexander

d n english

Dr. Danny Winbush

Mrs. Louise Stevens

Tim Batross

Lisa Coleman

Mrs. Virginia Dickinson

Linda Higgins

Samuel and Andrew Downs

Monita Carlin

Betty Curlin

Much gratitude is given to Mrs. Louise Stevens who spent years collecting material and presented it as a gift to Big Black Creek Historical, and to the family of Mr. Fonville who have helped with his stories.

Big Black Creek Historical Association
P.O. Box 50
Denmark, Tennessee
www.bigblackcreekhistorical.com
Face Book: Big Black Creek

Billy J. King
561 Hwy. 138
Denmark, Tennessee 38391
Bking49166@aol.com
731-427-7897

THE BIG BLACK CREEK HISTORICAL ASSOCIATION IS A NOT FOR PROFIT 501(C)3 FOUNDATION SUPPORTED BY GIFTS FROM FRIENDS LIKE YOU. YOUR DONATIONS ARE TAX DEDUCTIBLE.

IF YOU WOULD LIKE TO HELP WITH THIS WORK MAKE YOUR CHECKS PAYABEL TO BIG BLACK CREEK HISTORICAL

P.O. OFFICE BOX 50
DENMARK, TENNESSEE 38391

THANKS FOR YOUR SUPPORT AND HELP.

Main Street Publishing, Inc.

206 E. Main Street, Suite 207

P O Box 696

Jackson, TN 38301

Toll Free #: 866-457-7379

or

Local #: 731-427-7379

Visit us on the web:

www.mainstreetpublishing.com

www.mspbooks.com

E-Mail: editor@mainstreetpublishing.com